Spiritual Awakening for Geeks

Volume 1

Spiritual Awakening for Geeks

✦❈✦

Volume 1

Cultivating Mindfulness and Insight through Meditation

Jacob Gotwals

HUMAN POTENTIAL ARTS
SANTA FE, NM

Human Potential Arts LLC
Santa Fe, New Mexico
humanpotentialarts.com

21 20 19 18 17   1 2 3 4 5 6 7

ISBN: 978-0-9773610-3-8 (paperback)
Library of Congress Control Number: 2017909245

Library of Congress subject headings:
Meditation.
Spiritual life.

Yana Kligule designed the "eye" graphic and
other elements of this book's cover.

To my mentors and teachers, whose compassionate guidance has supported my spiritual journey.

CONTENTS

PREFACE

SPIRITUAL AWAKENING FOR GEEKS was born in 2014 as a website, blog, and newsletter where I started publishing my perspectives on awakening and spiritual practice. I added infrastructure to support an online community in 2015, and by 2016 this community had a number of active members. The material in this book was first published as a series of blog articles; I iteratively refined these articles based on feedback from the community (and feedback from mentors) before integrating the articles in this book.

As I describe in the introduction, I view awakening as a process of evolution that involves many aspects of human development. This book focuses on mindfulness and insight practices, which primarily catalyze changes in our attention, cognition, perception, and sense of self. Note that there are other important aspects of human development (for instance, compassion, emotional intelligence, and social intelligence) that are not directly addressed by mindfulness and insight practices; in the future, I may publish additional volumes in the *Spiritual Awakening for Geeks* series to address other aspects of awakening.

The process of writing has become an integral part of my spiritual life. I value writing from experience; my aspiration to write about deeper levels of mindfulness and insight has challenged me to practice with more dedication so that I can experience those levels more consistently, myself. Also, the process of writing has helped immensely in clarifying my own views, and holding clearer views has helped me practice more effectively. Trying to write about a subject is a great way to uncover one's lack of clarity about it!

⁂

My spiritual journey wouldn't have been possible without the compassionate support of many teachers and spiritual mentors. I'd like to acknowledge a number of people (and communities) who have supported my spiritual journey—either directly (through our interaction) or indirectly (through their published work). These acknowledgments are listed in approximate chronological order (from my earlier influences to my more recent ones). These acknowledgments are simply expressions of my gratitude. (When specific people or institutions are mentioned in this book, this is for informational purposes only; this is not intended to imply endorsement or sponsorship by these people or institutions.)

Marshall Rosenberg and other mentors and colleagues in the Nonviolent Communication community helped me cultivate empathy and compassion, gave me my first spiritual practices, and connected me with the work of Ken Wilber. The published work of Ken Wilber and his Integral community gave me models for integrating science, psychology, and spirituality, inspired me to seek spiritual insight, and connected me with the Karma Kagyu lineage. The Karma Kagyu lineage of Tibetan Buddhism, the Albuquerque Karma Thegsum Choling Tibetan Buddhist center, and the teachers and mentors I interacted with there gave me my first tastes of insight. The published work of Buddhist teacher Ken McLeod helped me deepen my experience and understanding of insight and intuition. Buddhist teacher George Draffan helped me deepen my capacity for concentration, and books by B. Alan Wallace *(The Attention Revolution)* and Shaila Catherine *(Wisdom Wide and Deep)* gave me helpful frameworks for understanding and practicing concentration. Meditation instructor Kenneth Folk helped me expand my experience of insight and clarify my understanding of it. The members of the Spiritual Awakening for Geeks community have inspired me to deeper levels of commitment to spiritual practice, writing, and teaching; they've also provided invaluable feed-back that has helped immensely in the process of revising and clari-fying the contents of this book. A number of additional authors and teachers who have influenced my work are named in the body of this book and in the bibliography.

INTRODUCTION

S OME OF US are called toward a journey of awakening. What does the call of awakening feel like? Yearning intensely for something you don't fully comprehend, with a curiosity you can't fully explain. Trying to grasp something that seems just out of reach. Knowing what's important to explore next, but not knowing why. Realizing that if you *don't* heed the call of awakening —if you instead decide to stay safe, in familiar territory—you'll be condemning your soul to a slow death.

The journey of awakening can be challenging. It's a personal journey; you're the only one who can hear *your* call of awakening, so you're the only one who can discern where it leads. On this journey, neither the destination nor the route is clear. You come across guides who claim to know the way—but you don't know whether they can be trusted or whether they've even *been* where you're trying to go. You encounter institutions that offer their support—but you wonder how effective their support actually is. Even when you find trustworthy guides, the value that they offer may be hidden behind dense jargon—often in a foreign language.

I've encountered all the above challenges on my own journey of awakening. However, I've persevered, and I'm glad to report that I seem to have made some progress on my journey. Through years of study and practice—with guidance and support from like-minded mentors and fellow travelers—I've been awakening to greater vitality, mindfulness, insight, intuition, and compassion. This process has radically shifted my understandings of self, life, and reality. It's also helped strengthen my self-awareness and emotional intelligence, empowering me and opening the door to more joy and peace of mind in my life.

Based on my experience, I believe awakening is possible for ordinary people like us (it's not just for spiritual superstars), awakening is possible without long retreats (in other words, awakening can and should be integrated into daily life), and awakening shouldn't require learning a foreign language or difficult spiritual jargon.

THE SPIRITUAL AWAKENING FOR GEEKS PROJECT

This book is part of the Spiritual Awakening for Geeks project; this project is my attempt to make the spiritual journey faster and easier for people who share my spiritual values and interests. The mission of Spiritual Awakening for Geeks is to provide clear, coherent, practical approaches to awakening—approaches that aren't tied to any particular religion or spiritual tradition. If you're familiar with psychology and the contemplative branches of the world's religions, you'll feel at home here; however, you don't have to be religious to benefit from Spiritual Awakening for Geeks. If you *are* practicing within a particular religion or spiritual tradition, I hope Spiritual Awakening for Geeks may give you helpful new perspectives on your spiritual journey.

In addition to providing guidance on awakening, Spiritual Awakening for Geeks also provides spiritual community. If you've felt like a misfit in the spiritual communities you've explored, you're not alone; many rational, spiritually-conscious people like you and me face the same problem. Most spiritual communities simply aren't a good match for us, because we're different from the average seeker in a number of ways:

- **We're rational.** We want a community of open-minded critical thinkers.
- **We're practical.** We want effective practices—not just philosophy.
- **We're discerning.** We're looking for clarity and insight—not just peace.
- **We're self-directed.** We're not interested in handing our lives over to gurus or spiritual institutions.

If this sounds like you, then welcome home! If you don't consider yourself a geek, that's okay—come on in anyway. (Your "inner geek" will appreciate it.) I use the term *geek* affectionately and proudly—not pejoratively. I've addressed this work toward geeks because, in my experience (as a self-proclaimed geek), my fellow geeks tend to share the values I've listed above. Also, I believe many geeks appreciate a good adventure—and I take an adventurous, exploratory approach to spiritual practice.

There's more to Spiritual Awakening for Geeks than this book. Visit spiritualawakeningforgeeks.com to connect with our supportive community and discover the latest developments in the Spiritual Awakening for Geeks project. Resources specific to this book are at spiritualawakeningforgeeks.com/firstvolume.

FOUNDATIONAL PRINCIPLES

I've based the Spiritual Awakening for Geeks project on several foundational principles; these are reflected in how I've chosen to write this book. Since I value clarity, I write in plain English, defining the terms I use and avoiding jargon as much as possible. (Note that this book includes a comprehensive glossary.) I want my work to be practical (not just theoretical or philosophical), so my writing is geared toward practice and personal transformation. I want my work to be useful to people who have busy lives, who are engaged in the world—so daily life (rather than extended retreat) is the primary context for the practices I recommend. I value an open, flexible, self-guided approach to spiritual practice. I don't claim any special authority (other than the authority gained through personal experience), and I believe *you* should have authority over—and responsibility for—your own spiritual journey. I don't claim that this book is comprehensive, and I don't claim that the approach I describe is the only way—or the best way—to cultivate mindfulness and insight; it's just been *my* way. I hope it might be helpful to you as you find *your* way.

I value diversity and autonomy in spiritual practice, and my writing is informed by my experiences with a diversity of mentors, teachers, and traditions. I reference and acknowledge many of these sources in this book, and I provide a bibliography for those interested in exploring these sources in greater depth. I hope this book will be helpful to people practicing in a wide range of contexts. However, the views expressed in this book are my own; they are not intended to represent the views of any other persons, traditions, religions, lineages, organizations, or professions that I may be associated with. Writing from an independent stance gives me maximum freedom to express myself clearly, drawing on existing forms when useful and defining new forms as needed.

This book is not intended to be a comprehensive source of information; however, it *is* intended to articulate a clear, self-consistent system for cultivating mindfulness and insight that can serve as a starting point for further exploration. I've tried to explicitly relate aspects of this system to aspects of other systems; I hope this will make this book more useful for those who are practicing within other systems, and I hope it will help you leverage your knowledge of other systems to better understand this system. For further exploration, see the sources listed in the bibliography.

While I've received some positive feedback about this book, as of this writing, I haven't validated the effectiveness of the approaches in this book in any methodical way (other than through personal experience). As I find more evidence of the effectiveness of

these   approaches,   I'll   publish   this   at
spiritualawakeningforgeeks.com.

MY JOURNEY OF AWAKENING

Since this book is based on personal experience, it seems important
to summarize my experiences with awakening and the evolution of
my views on awakening; I do so in this section. My understanding
of awakening has evolved over the course of my life and has
changed dramatically a number of times. (I describe parts of my
journey in more detail in my book *Tricksters in the Desert*.)

SCIENCE AND HUMANISM

As a teenager and a young adult, I loved thunderstorms, fractals,
and computers. I saw magic in nature, technology, and chaos theory. I saw myself primarily as a *physical* being existing in the *natural* world. Science (the rational study of nature) was my unofficial
religion, and humanism was the basis of my worldview. If I
thought about spiritual awakening at all, it was with scientific skep-
ticism.

I was also starting to become aware of awareness. I was curious
and perplexed about how awareness *fits in* with nature—but I
wouldn't find much support for exploring this for about twenty
years.

NONVIOLENT COMMUNICATION

In my late twenties, a self-help practice called Nonviolent Communication (NVC) caught my attention. This practice was created by
psychologist Marshall Rosenberg who was a student of humanistic
psychologist Carl Rogers. The aim of NVC is to cultivate compassion by focusing attention on feelings and human needs.

After being parched dry by the relentless hyper-intellectual focus of computer science and Silicon Valley, NVC's focus on emotions and relationships came as a welcome relief. I adopted NVC as my first spiritual practice, and I started seeing myself primarily as an *emotional* being existing in a *relational* world; NVC became my primary frame of reference for making sense of life. I viewed awakening as the process of learning to recognize our feelings and needs and learning to let go of patterns of thought and communication that make it difficult to recognize and honor our needs.

INTEGRAL THEORY

I started meditating in my thirties—mostly for stress reduction. Around that time, I discovered the work of philosopher Ken Wilber. He expressed himself both in the language of science and psychology (which I was familiar with) and the language of mystical spirituality (which was new to me). His work bridged those two cultures, making a personal exploration of mysticism possible for me for the first time in my life.

I was captivated by Wilber's work, and I consumed it voraciously. His Integral Theory (which unites science, psychology, and mysticism) became my new frame of reference for making sense of life. I started viewing myself as an *evolving* consciousness existing on a *mystical* ground of being, and I started viewing awakening the recognition of that ground. I didn't *understand* that ground, but I was determined to make sense of it and experience it for myself. I turned to the world's mystical traditions for guidance.

TIBETAN BUDDHISM

In my early forties, after floundering around for a few years exploring several mystical traditions that weren't good matches for me, I finally discovered the Karma Kagyu lineage of Tibetan Buddhism. I was delighted by the simplicity and clarity of the teachings of this lineage. I started exploring them deeply—first through a local practice center, then later through the published work of Buddhist teacher Ken McLeod.

Over the course of three years, I investigated self and subjective experience through various meditation practices intended to foster insight. These practices uprooted my remaining materialist biases and shifted my sense of self. This work was exciting, invigorating, and sometimes disturbing. My attention shifted toward the mysterious, perfect, luminous union of awareness and subjective experience, which I viewed as the ultimate ground of being. I viewed awakening as the recognition of that ground, and I recognized all phenomena (including conceptual frames of reference) as arisings in (and as) that ground. Intuitive knowing became my guide, and my intellect became a servant of my intuition.

REVISITING AWARENESS

In my mid-forties, I met meditation instructor Kenneth Folk. After about five minutes of conversation, Kenneth told me he could see where my practice had gotten stuck. I was flustered by this comment; I didn't understand what he meant. I suspected that either he had a defect in *his* practice, or a misunderstanding had arisen between us.

Later that night, my attention returned to what Kenneth had said. Intent on being completely honest with myself, I looked closely at the only place where my practice could *possibly* be stuck: the union of awareness and experience. I soon recognized that I'd become identified with the concept of *awareness*. (This had given rise to a telltale fundamentalist zeal and defensiveness about my preferred frame of reference; Kenneth had probably picked up on this during our brief conversation.)

This recognition disrupted my sense of self, leaving me feeling disturbed and disembodied for a few hours. However, I woke up the next morning feeling surprisingly relaxed and free. Later, as I integrated this experience, I realized that I still viewed the union of awareness and experience as a useful frame of reference, but I no longer viewed it (or any other frame of reference) as *ultimate*. This transformation freed up my energy, allowing me to respond more flexibly and creatively to life.

AWAKENING AS A PROCESS OF EVOLUTION

So, which of the above shifts in consciousness were *real* spiritual awakenings? In my opinion, *all of them* were important awakenings because *spiritual awakening*, as I define it, is the evolution of consciousness toward greater wisdom and compassion. As we awaken, we grow both more empowered and more likely to use our power for good. We grow both more able and more willing to serve the well-being of all.

This definition of awakening is intentionally quite broad. In some spiritual traditions, the term *awakening* is used more specifically—to refer to the attainment of particular states of mind or particular levels of development. I prefer to define awakening as a process of evolution (rather than an attainment); this demystifies awakening (by allowing it to be defined in terms that everyone can understand) and democratizes it (by allowing us to view awakening as something we've all been participating in, all our lives).

Of course, having terminology to refer to particular states of mind and levels of development is also important and useful. However, in my opinion, it's important for a spiritual path to be grounded in down-to-earth intentions that can be understood by all and that are clearly connected to human needs. Otherwise, we risk becoming mere consciousness technicians, aspiring toward abstract goals that are disconnected from life.

THE MANY ASPECTS OF AWAKENING

As I see it, awakening involves many lines of human development; I've listed some of them below. (I don't intend this to be a *complete* list.) As we awaken:

- Our **attention** may grow stronger; we may become less subject to distraction.
- Our **will** may grow stronger; we may become less driven by impulse and habit.
- Our **perception** may grow clearer; we may perceive life more fully and vividly, and we may learn to recognize an increasingly wide set of phenomena.
- Our **cognition** may become more powerful, less biased, more flexible, and more discerning.
- Our **sense of self** may shift as we recognize misperceptions about ourselves.
- Our **intuition** may grow more accurate and accessible.
- Our **vitality** may increase.
- Our **psychological health** may improve.
- Our **emotional center of gravity** may shift (from anxiety toward peace of mind, for instance).
- Our **emotional and social intelligence** may increase.
- Our **morality** may shift (from egocentric concern for our own well-being toward concern for the well-being of successively larger and more diverse groups).

This implies that there are many aspects of awakening, there are many degrees of awakening, it's possible to be more awake in some ways than in others, and it's possible for our degree of awakening to fluctuate over time. For instance, in my case, even though I believe I've experienced some important awakenings, I still "fall asleep" (and re-awaken) regularly, and I imagine (and hope!) I may have more awakenings ahead.

I've often encountered a different, more monolithic view of awakening: the view that awakening is all-or-nothing (either you're awake or you're not), permanent (once awake, always awake), and absolute (those who have awakened can do no wrong). To me, this view of awakening seems dangerously simplistic.

By adopting the view that awakening involves multiple lines of development and that an individual who is highly evolved on some lines may simultaneously be quite unevolved on other lines, we can make sense of some seemingly bizarre phenomena that show up on a regular basis—for instance, highly credentialed spiritual teachers who regularly abuse and take advantage of their students. (In these cases, we might suspect deficiencies in their psychological health, emotional intelligence, social intelligence, and/or moral development—while still allowing for high levels of development in other lines.) (I've adopted the terminology of *lines, levels,* and *states* from philosopher Ken Wilber's Integral Theory. His work has also influenced my views on the evolution of consciousness.)

THE DIVERSE FACES OF AWAKENING

If spiritual awakening is a process of evolution, then we can define *a spiritual awakening* as a *step* in that process. A spiritual awakening is a qualitative (rather than a quantitative) shift in consciousness— usually, a shift that's experienced for the first time. For instance, strengthening one's attention can be an important aspect of awakening—but when my attention gets a bit stronger, I probably wouldn't call that a spiritual awakening. However, if my newfound strength of attention allows me to witness my stream of thoughts for the first time (without getting distracted by their content), I might call *that* a spiritual awakening.

It can be difficult to imagine what a given qualitative shift in consciousness will be like until we've actually experienced it. For this reason, the awakenings that we have not yet experienced tend to seem mysterious and alluring—and conversely, the awakenings that we have *already* experienced tend to seem mundane. When you're in the process of cultivating insight, it may not seem like much of a spiritual awakening when someone in a recovery program puts their faith in a higher power for the first time; however, in my view, both of these can be important and authentic forms of awakening.

Do all spiritual paths lead to the same destination? Yes and no. To the extent that any spiritual path is authentic, it will tend to foster awakening. However, different traditions emphasize different spiritual practices, which affect different lines of development (and attract different types of practitioners). For instance, some traditions emphasize love and compassion, others emphasize insight and clarity, and others emphasize energy and vitality. This means that awakening can look and feel quite different in different spiritual traditions.

BEYOND INDIVIDUAL AWAKENING

So far, I've been discussing awakening in relation to individuals. I believe it's also important to consider awakening in broader terms. Can relationships, cultures, and social systems become more awakened? Sure, why not? Consider the following generalized definition: spiritual awakening is the evolution of *consciousness, relationships, cultures, and social systems* toward greater ability and propensity to serve the well-being of all.

In this book, my focus is on individual consciousness—but there's no reason we must limit ourselves to individuals. If we want to be effective in serving the well-being of all, it's important for us to foster awakened relationships, cultures, and social systems, as well. (Meditation instructor Kenneth Folk has applied Ken Wilber's concept of *quadrants* to spiritual awakening; these ideas have informed the views expressed in this section.)

FACETS OF AWAKENING

This book focuses on practices for cultivating mindfulness and insight. I view mindfulness and insight as *facets of awakening*, meaning that they are measures of awakening, faculties that result from awakening, and catalysts for further awakening. (In my model of awakening, facets of awakening are the top-level categories that I use to conceptualize awakening and to organize spiritual practices.) Mindfulness and insight each have a related set of practices; mindfulness practices work with our attention, and insight practices work with our cognition, perception, and sense of self.

Note that many important aspects of human development (for instance, compassion and emotional/social intelligence) aren't directly addressed by mindfulness and insight practices—so there's more to awakening than cultivating mindfulness and insight! I hope you will explore beyond this book to discover additional aspects of awakening that you feel drawn toward.

SUMMARY

This book is part of the *Spiritual Awakening for Geeks* project, which aims to provide spiritual community and clear, coherent, practical approaches to spiritual awakening—approaches that aren't associated with any particular religion or spiritual tradition. As I define it, *spiritual awakening* is the evolution of consciousness toward greater wisdom and compassion. There are many aspects of awakening, there are many degrees of awakening, it's possible to be more awake in some ways than in others, and it's possible for our degree of awakening to fluctuate over time. In addition to cultivating our individual awakening, I believe it's important to foster awakened relationships, cultures, and social systems, as well. This book focuses on meditation practices for cultivating mindfulness and insight, which I view as two *facets of awakening*.

❧

Part 1 of this book *("Prepare for the Journey")* leads you through the basics of creating a spiritual practice routine and learning how to meditate. Part 2 *("Cultivate Mindfulness")* shows how to use concentration and other meditation practices to cultivate mindfulness (a stable, clear, expansive awareness of a wide range of your current experiences). Part 3 *("Cultivate Insight")* builds on this foundation, showing how to use additional meditation practices to transcend self and reality by cultivating insight (an experiential understanding of the relationships between self, reality, awareness, and subjective experience). Let the journey begin!

PART ONE

PREPARE FOR THE JOURNEY

CHAPTER 1

CULTIVATE VITALITY

TO GET IN SHAPE for awakening, you must cultivate *vitality* (which I consider to be a facet of awakening, like mindfulness and insight). Cultivating vitality involves improving your well-being and empowering yourself. As your vitality increases, you become more efficient; you can create more value with less effort. I experience vitality as a sense of relaxed, energized openness; vitality feels *good!*

THE IMPORTANCE OF VITALITY

Vitality is required for awakening because embarking on a spiritual journey requires surplus energy—energy that's not tied up in other activities. To illustrate this, consider an analogy: let's say you have a job you don't like, and you don't have any surplus energy (in the form of time or money). Even though you don't like your job, you'll have a hard time leaving it, because all your available resources are tied up in your current pattern of living. However, if you have some surplus energy, you can use it to start cultivating other income sources; that makes it more likely that you'll be able to leave your job, eventually.

Awakening is similar. Getting started on a spiritual journey requires energy; for instance, energy is required both to learn about awakening and to do spiritual practices. Building your vitality can help you create the surplus energy you need to *get started* on your spiritual journey, and once you've gotten started, cultivating vitality helps you make *more efficient progress* on your journey. As a side benefit, the surplus energy you create can be used to fuel positive transformations in other areas of your life, as well.

In my experience, as one awakens, one becomes both a more powerful collector and a more efficient transformer of energy. Eventually, one can reach a tipping point at which one's awakening process starts to *liberate* more energy than it consumes; at this point, awakening becomes a self-sustaining process, like a success-ful entrepreneurial venture or a tree you've planted that finally gets established. So, in a broad sense, cultivating *any aspect of awakening* can be viewed as a means of cultivating vitality. (For an example of how vitality can be increased by cultivating mindfulness, see the section "Tension Releases and Energy Surges" in chapter 8.)

PRACTICES FOR CULTIVATING VITALITY

If you're just getting started on your spiritual journey, there are many basic ways to get your body, mind, and life in shape for the journey—none of which require any advanced skills. Here's a list of some basic intentions and practices I've found helpful for cultivat-ing vitality:

- **Care for your physical health.** Stay up-to-date on health news and get professional support when you need it.
- **Get your work life and financial life in order.** Awakening gets a lot easier when you're less worried about money.
- **Develop habits that support your well-being** and let go of habits that don't.
- **Relax your body.** Stretching and massage can be great for this. Try self-massage, trading massages, or getting profes-sional massages.

- **Engage your body.** Exercise. Find a yoga class, or learn at home (like I did) through books and videos. Try qigong and ecstatic movement.
- **Cultivate supportive relationships.** These could be family relationships, friendships, informal or formal support groups, or other types of intimate relationships. Intimate relationships can be challenging, so don't hesitate to seek professional support when you need it.
- **Heal emotional pain and trauma.** I've found self-help approaches to healing to be helpful, including breathwork. Psychotherapy can be helpful, too—both for individual issues and for relationship issues. Spiritual practice can cause latent emotional issues to surface; for this reason, I believe that psychotherapy can be an important and useful complement to spiritual practice—even for people who have no major psychological problems. If you can, try to find a psychotherapist who has some familiarity with meditation and who has a view of spirituality that's compatible with yours.

(I don't intend the list above to be comprehensive; also, keep in mind that some activities on this list may not be appropriate for your situation.)

You're probably already aware of various areas of your life that could use some attention. If you're unsure how to address issues that are holding back your vitality, do some research online or at your favorite bookstore or seek professional guidance.

CREATING A SPIRITUAL PRACTICE ROUTINE

A *spiritual practice* is an activity that you engage in to help you awaken. A *spiritual practice routine* is a set of spiritual practices that you make a habit of doing regularly. If you don't already have a spiritual practice routine, creating one is one of the best things you can do to support both your awakening and your general well-being.

If you're creating a practice routine for the first time, I suggest you focus on cultivating vitality. Choose a set of intentions and practices from the list above (or choose different ones, if you want), clarify the specific practices you want to do regularly, create an initial practice schedule—then get started on your practices! As you gain experience with your practice routine, you can make adjustments to both your schedule and your practices, as necessary.

As an example, as of this writing, I do the following practices for cultivating vitality: gentle stretching in the morning when I get out of bed, qigong in the morning and at night before bed, physical exercise (cardiovascular exercise and weight lifting) three times a week; yoga on the days when I don't exercise; and an extended breathwork session and ecstatic movement whenever I feel the need (often every few weeks). I view relationships as an important source of support, and I view *being in* relationship as a powerful spiritual practice, so I invest significant time and energy cultivating relationships with family, friends, and colleagues. I also seek psychotherapy when I need additional emotional support. If all this sounds overwhelming, don't worry—you get to create a practice routine that works for *you*. If that means doing just one or two practices a few times a week, that's fine.

OVERCOMING INERTIA

It can be difficult to overcome inertia when you're starting a spiritual practice routine. Life settles into patterns, and our patterns take on a life of their own that can be very resistant to change. Because of this, it can be difficult to start meditating, exercising, or doing any other spiritual practice.

To overcome this inertia, take one small step at a time. Rather than focusing on the big picture (for instance, starting a daily meditation practice), temporarily forget the big picture and just ask yourself, "What's the next step I could take, right now, toward practice?" Perhaps it's to change into your exercise clothes. Do that step, then repeat (again, ask yourself, "What's the next step?" and do it). The smaller you can make these steps, the better. It's not so hard to take one small step at a time, and focusing on the next step (instead of the big picture) prevents you from getting over-whelmed. I've found this process very effective for starting many kinds of difficult-to-start activities.

You may think there's no space in your life for spiritual practice —and therefore, you can't do it. It may be true that there's no space in your life for spiritual practice, but that doesn't mean you can't do it; it just means you need to make space for it! Making space for it will require cutting back on something else. This is all about priori-ties; if awakening is important to you, you'll make space for it.

Summary

Cultivating *vitality* involves improving your well-being and em-powering yourself. Vitality is required for awakening, and awaken-ing increases vitality. Eventually, your awakening process can start to liberate more energy than it consumes; at this point, awakening becomes a self-sustaining process.

A *spiritual practice* is an activity that you engage in to help you awaken. A *spiritual practice routine* is a set of spiritual practices that you make a habit of doing regularly. If you don't already have a spiritual practice routine, creating one is one of the best things you can do to support both your awakening and your general well-be-ing. It can be difficult to start doing any spiritual practice; to over-come this inertia, take one small step at a time. If there's no space in your life for spiritual practice, make space for it.

If you're creating a practice routine for the first time, focus on cultivating vitality. There are many basic ways to cultivate vitality; some of these are listed in this chapter. The next chapter describes how to incorporate meditation into your spiritual practice routine.

Chapter 2

Learn How to Meditate

A S I DEFINE IT, *meditation* is any practice that involves directing your attention toward your current subjective experience. Meditation is a workhorse of spiritual practice; it can be used to cultivate many facets of awakening, including mindfulness and insight. What facets you cultivate depends on the specific meditation practices you do. This chapter describes a general framework for meditation that you can use as a basis for many different meditation practices.

Meditation Postures

In my view, there's no one "right" meditation posture. Below, I've described a few postures that work for me—but everyone is different, so do some research, experiment, and find postures that work for you. (Searching online for "meditation posture" should give you some ideas.) Give yourself permission to modify the "standard" postures to make them work better for you. (My leg muscles have always been tight no matter how much I've tried to stretch them, so I've done plenty of experimentation and modification myself over the years.)

Here's an important caution. As you learn new meditation postures, you may be putting your body in positions it hasn't been in before. To do this in a healthy way, gently stretch your body *before* meditating and monitor your level of discomfort *while* you're meditating. You shouldn't feel pain while meditating or getting into a meditation posture; pain is your body's way of telling you you're pushing too hard. I'm not an expert on physical health, but I believe that regularly meditating in a painful posture is likely to cause damage to your body over time. Some spiritual traditions have macho, stoical cultures in which an ability to endure pain while meditating is valued; I don't think this is beneficial. I know of two meditation teachers who eventually developed serious knee problems; don't be like them! Consult a health professional if you have any questions or concerns.

Meditation requires a balance between relaxation and attentiveness. Neither relaxation nor attentiveness is supported by high levels of discomfort. Learning a few different postures allows you to switch postures in the midst of a meditation session when you get uncomfortable. When I'm doing a long session, I tend to rotate through my favorite postures; I find that changing posture every 30 to 60 minutes works well for me. The following are a few of my favorite postures.

SITTING IN A CHAIR

For those new to meditation, I recommend sitting in a chair because it's the simplest and easiest way to get started. Armless office chairs can work well for this; the height of the chair is important and office chairs usually have adjustable height, which is helpful. I adjust the height so that my upper legs are angled straight or slightly down. I sit with my palms resting on my thighs, my back erect, and a natural curve in my lower back. I tuck my chin down ever so slightly, which makes my upper back more comfortable.

I've done several variations of this posture. In one, I scoot forward a bit on the chair, resting my thighs on the edge of the chair and crossing my ankles under the chair. In another, I sit farther back in the chair with my feet flat on the floor in front of me and my rear end touching the back of the chair (so my back isn't actually touching the back of the chair, just my rear end).

As of this writing, my favorite meditation posture involves putting a meditation cushion on a low chair and sitting on the cushion with my feet flat on the floor; I find that this posture requires the same level of balance as sitting cross-legged on a cushion, but without the knee strain of a cross-legged posture. (Balancing on a cushion seems to be helpful in maintaining the relaxed alertness required for meditation.)

For my cushion, I used a round meditation cushion filled with buckwheat hulls from DharmaCrafts. I've used kapok-filled cushions, but I found that the buckwheat hulls gave me better support and allowed me to adjust the height of the cushion by adding or removing hulls. I needed a fairly high cushion in order to sit comfortably, and I added extra hulls over time as the original ones compacted. Just as with postures, I suggest you experiment with different types of cushions, benches, and other meditation supports to discover what works best for you.

My neck and back muscles get tired sometimes when I'm meditating in a sitting posture (either in a chair or cross-legged); to stretch my neck and back, I place the palms of my hands on the top part of my upper thighs with the fingers of each hand pointing toward each other, I make fists with my hands (leaving the top part of my palms on my thighs), then I straighten my arms to push my fists against my thighs. This raises my shoulders and stretches my shoulders and back.

SITTING CROSS-LEGGED

My favorite posture used to be sitting cross-legged with my rear end on a meditation cushion, one foot on the floor, the other resting on my opposite calf, and both knees on the floor. *However, I don't recommend sitting cross-legged unless you can do it comfortably, without knee pain.* Personally, I can't maintain this posture for more than 30 minutes or so without getting uncomfortable—and I recently stopped using this posture entirely after discovering that it was giving me knee pain between sessions. I'm now finding that sitting in a chair works just as well for me, and my knees are much happier.

When I was using this posture, to cushion my ankles, I'd put the meditation cushion on a bed, couch, or meditation mat (which served as the "floor"). I put my palms on my thighs, I let my spine be relaxed but erect, and I tucked my chin down ever so slightly to support my back. I sat slightly off-center on the cushion so that my torso felt balanced; if my right foot was on top, I shifted slightly left on the cushion (and vice versa).

LYING DOWN

Another posture I use sometimes is lying on my back on a rug with a low cushion under my knees, a small pillow under my head, and my hands resting on my thighs. An alternative is lying in bed, either on my back or on my side. If I lie on my side, I put my head on a pillow, my upper hand on my upper leg, and my lower hand either under the pillow or next to it.

Meditating while lying down seems to work best after I've been meditating for a while in a sitting posture; otherwise, it's too easy for me to fall asleep. However, I frequently use this posture for meditating in bed in the morning before I get up (without meditating while sitting up first); this creates a gentle transition from sleep into waking life.

WALKING

When I've been meditating for a while and I'm ready to shift postures, I sometimes do a walking meditation posture to stretch my legs first. I walk around the edge of the room, taking steps slowly and deliberately, placing one foot directly in front of the other, with palms together and fingers pointed upward at heart level. This requires attention and balance—and this, in turn, helps me focus.

Preparing for a Meditation Session

If possible, meditate in a setting where you won't be disturbed. It's not that you *shouldn't* meditate in a busy, chaotic environment—it's just that a chaotic environment makes meditation a lot more challenging. On the other hand, when my schedule is such that I can't meditate in a peaceful environment, I get my meditation in whenever and wherever I can. (For instance, I've had many good meditation sessions on the train and in airports.) Make spiritual practice a priority by turning off devices that may interrupt your session.

Set an intention for how long your session will be, and consider setting a timer to gently notify you when your session time is over. The benefits of using a timer are:

1. you don't have to keep track of time during your session, and
2. you'll be less tempted to end your session early.

I used a timer regularly while I was learning to meditate, but at a certain point, meditation got pleasant enough that I was no longer tempted to stop my sessions early; at that point, using a timer started seeming less important.

If you're learning a new meditation practice, review the instructions for that practice before your session so you won't have to refer to them during your session. (I give instructions for a basic meditation practice in the section below.)

Meditating

If you're new to meditation, I suggest you make cultivating mindfulness—via concentration meditation—the initial focus of your meditation sessions. I cover mindfulness and concentration in detail in part 2, "Cultivate Mindfulness;" however, as a starting point, below are instructions for a basic concentration meditation practice. This is a good practice to work with as you learn how to meditate.

1. Choose an object of attention.
   a) For many people, it works well to focus on the abdominal sensations of breathing and count breaths. (I like to count to eight then start over. Put most of your attention on the sensations of breathing—not on the counting.)
   b) For others, it works well to place a small object on the floor a comfortable distance in front of you and focus on its visual appearance.
2. Attempt to rest your attention on the object of attention you've chosen.
3. Eventually, you'll notice that you're completely distracted (probably lost in thought) and that your attention is no longer on your chosen object. At this point, gently return your attention to your chosen object and go back to step 2.

When you're ready to start meditating, assume a relaxed, comfortable meditation posture. Start your timer (if you're using one), then follow the instructions for the specific meditation practice you're doing until your session time is over.

MOVEMENT VERSUS STILLNESS

For effective meditation, it's important to be alert—yet also relaxed and comfortable. Meditation shouldn't be an endurance test or a competition. Try to strike a balance between overly-rigid stillness and overly-permissive fidgeting. Avoiding fidgeting helps calm your body and mind, and avoiding being overly rigid helps your body and mind relax.

If your body wants (or needs) to move, let it move. (I make a distinction between movement and distracted fidgeting.) For instance, as I go deeper into meditation, I often start noticing areas of tension in my body. As my attention rests on those areas of tension, the tension gets released. As this happens, I often find that my arms want to shake—so I let them shake (rather than trying to hold them still). Obviously, this works better when I'm meditating alone than when I'm meditating in a group setting; in a group, I try to be less active to avoid disturbing others.

THINKING LATER

Often, when I'm in the midst of concentration meditation, I start thinking—and it feels *natural*. It feels like something I *want* to do and am *choosing* to do. Thinking is such a strong habit that I don't even *notice* that it's not in line with my intention to focus my attention on my chosen object.

To solve this problem, I find that it helps to explicitly clarify that for the duration of my meditation session, thinking is *not* what I'm intending to do. (This is different than trying not to think; I'm not *trying not* to think, I'm just clarifying that any thinking that I *do* find myself doing is unintentional and involuntary.)

As a simple way of reminding myself of this, I'll sometimes start a meditation session by reminding myself, "Think *later!*" Then, when I find myself thinking during my session, it becomes more clear that my thinking is an unwelcome intrusion (rather than the productive endeavor I generally assume it to be). Many ideas may come to mind during your meditation sessions. If they're worth remembering, you won't forget them—so make a mental note of them and postpone recording them until your session is over.

REFLECTING ON A MEDITATION SESSION

Learn to be your own guru! I believe this is important, even if you're working with teachers and mentors. After you meditate, consider what you hoped to experience and what you actually experienced. Identify your unanswered questions and clarify your intentions for future meditation sessions. You can do this as a self-reflective mental exercise or in writing. Writing in a journal can help you integrate things you've learned during your session and help you clarify intentions for future sessions.

MEDITATING DAILY

Meditation is most effective when done consistently, so I suggest you make meditation a daily part of your spiritual practice routine. Start with a schedule you can do consistently, even if it's one brief session per day. (When I first started meditating, I started with one five-minute session per day.)

If you have a limited amount of time per day to meditate, there are two ways to go: you can use all your time for one long session, or you can spread it across several short sessions. I suggest you experiment with both of these approaches. The benefit of one long session is that you have more time to go deeper. The benefit of several short sessions is that there will be a shorter period of time between sessions; to some extent, this allows you to pick up where you left off in the previous session.

As you get comfortable meditating, gradually increase the frequency and length of your meditation sessions. Try to get to a point at which you do three sessions per day, and try to make at least one of your sessions is 45 to 60 minutes long. Meditation is supported by relaxation—and it takes time for the body to relax. I've found that often, something magical happens around 50 to 60 minutes into a meditation session. If you haven't tried meditating for that long yet, I suggest that you give it a try.

Early in the morning and late at night tend to be times when we're less likely to be disturbed, so these are generally good times to meditate. I try to meditate in the morning, in the evening before bed, and once in the middle of the day.

Summary

I define *meditation* as any practice that involves directing your attention toward your current subjective experience. Gently stretch your body before meditating and monitor your level of discomfort while you're meditating. You shouldn't feel pain while meditating or getting into a meditation posture; consult a health professional if you have any questions or concerns.

There's no one "right" meditation posture, so find postures that work for *you*. For those new to meditation, I recommend sitting in a chair because it's the simplest and easiest way to get started. I sit with my palms resting on my thighs, my back erect, and a natural curve in my lower back; I tuck my chin down ever so slightly. I don't recommend sitting cross-legged unless you can do it comfortably, without knee pain. Meditating while lying down seems to work best after I've been meditating for a while in a sitting posture; otherwise, it's too easy for me to fall asleep. When I've been meditating for a while and I'm ready to shift postures, I sometimes do a walking meditation to stretch my legs first.

Meditate in a setting where you won't be disturbed. Set an intention for how long your session will be, and consider setting a timer. For a basic concentration meditation practice, choose an object of attention (such as the abdominal sensations of breathing or an object on the floor in front of you). Attempt to rest your attention on the object of attention you've chosen. Eventually, you'll notice that you're completely distracted (probably lost in thought) and that your attention is no longer on your chosen object; gently return your attention to your chosen object. For effective meditation, it's important to be alert—yet also relaxed and comfortable; try to strike a balance between overly-rigid stillness and overly-permissive fidgeting. After you meditate, consider what you hoped to experience and what you actually experienced; identify your unanswered questions and clarify your intentions for future meditation sessions.

Meditation is most effective when done consistently, so make meditation a daily part of your spiritual practice routine. As you get comfortable meditating, gradually increase the frequency and length of your meditation sessions. Early in the morning and late at night tend to be times when we're less likely to be disturbed, so these are generally good times to meditate.

CHAPTER 3

EXPAND YOUR PRACTICE ROUTINE

I F YOU'VE BEEN FOLLOWING the guidance in this book, at this point, you have a basic spiritual practice routine which includes a number of practices for cultivating vitality as well as a daily meditation practice. This chapter explores ways you can vary and expand your practice routine.

PRACTICING WITH OTHERS

Many spiritual practices can be done with others. Try practicing with others occasionally, to see what that's like. In my experience, when I'm meditating with others, my meditation sessions tend to be deeper; that's been true both of in-person and of online group sessions. Being in a group makes it easier to connect with peers and mentors who can support your practice, and being in a group can create opportunities for you to contribute to the well-being of others, too. (You can connect with the Spiritual Awakening for Geeks community by visiting spiritualawakeningforgeeks.com.)

I've sometimes enjoyed weekly meditation sessions with local groups of meditators. It may take some searching to find a local group that you resonate with. You don't necessarily need a group whose focus matches yours exactly; you just need a group that's open-minded enough to let you do your own practices (or a group that does practices that you want to learn).

Competitiveness tends to be a problem when meditating in groups; for instance, it's easy to start feeling competitive about how long you can sit in a particular posture or how fast you are progressing toward particular goals. Don't succumb to these competitive feelings. Learn a few different meditation postures so you can change to a new posture when you get uncomfortable. If the group frowns on changing posture mid-session, consider finding a less rigid group to sit with.

You may find that it's easier to find an online group whose interests match yours than an in-person group; however, the drawback of online groups is that the "bandwidth" of connection is often a lot lower, due to the nature of online communication. However, technological advances have been improving the online group experience.

While practicing when others can have many benefits, try not to make your practice routine dependent on having other people to practice with; make sure you know how to practice independently, too.

PRACTICING IN DAILY LIFE

So far, I've mostly been discussing *formal practice sessions:* times set aside specifically for meditation or other forms of spiritual practice. Your spiritual practice routine can (and should) also include *informal practice* interspersed in your daily life; for instance, stretching while waiting at stoplights.

Informal practice can help you maintain momentum between formal practice sessions; it can also allow you to harvest some of the benefits of spiritual practice in the midst of daily life. Get creative and find ways to integrate your practices into your life. (As always, exercise caution when safety is an issue—for instance, when driving.)

TAKING RETREATS

In addition to your daily meditation routine, it's a good idea to make time for retreats occasionally, as well. A *retreat* is simply an extended period of time reserved for spiritual practice—*extended* meaning longer than what's usual for you in your daily practice routine. You can integrate any of your practices into your retreats, and different retreats can be focused on different practices.

A retreat doesn't have to take long. For instance, I do a mini-retreat every couple weeks in which I reserve a morning, afternoon, or evening for spiritual practice. Retreats don't have to be complicated or expensive, either. If your home environment supports it, you don't even have to leave home to do a retreat; I am a big fan of do-it-yourself, stay-at-home retreats. I've done a few day-long and weekend retreats at home that have been quite deep and effective. (As of yet, I don't have experience with longer retreats, though I look forward to exploring them sometime.)

To plan a stay-at-home retreat, choose a period of time when others in your household won't be around—or, at least, a time when others can give you some time and space to yourself. Plan a rough schedule in advance, with time set aside for a variety of spiritual practices, meals, breaks, and rest. By planning a schedule in advance, you won't need to make decisions in the midst of your retreat, so you'll be able to focus on your practices better. Consider cooking your meals ahead of time, so all you need to do is heat them up. (I'm grateful to Buddhist meditation teacher George Draffan for sharing his perspectives on stay-at-home retreats with me; his views have informed mine.)

Rest is an important part of a retreat. When you find yourself feeling fatigued, it's time to take a break. Go for a walk, or do something else peaceful that doesn't require much effort.

One caution about doing retreats on your own: solo retreats are more intense than retreats with others because interaction with others is a significant way that human beings regulate our emotions. When you're doing a retreat on your own, you'll lose an emotional support system that you probably take for granted, so be prepared to work with feelings that are more intense than usual. It's okay to end your retreat early if you find that you've bitten off more than you can chew.

I believe that generally, it's best to start learning how to meditate through a daily meditation practice that's integrated into your daily life; this creates a relatively gentle transition into states of increased mindfulness and insight. I don't think it's a good idea to jump into an intensive, multi-day meditation retreat without having had much experience with meditation; I believe this could be a shock to your system that could be harmful and could lead to unpleasant and distressing experiences.

SUMMARY

Many spiritual practices can be done with others; try practicing with others occasionally (for instance, you might do weekly meditation sessions with local groups of meditators). However, try not to make your practice routine *dependent* on having other people to practice with.

Times set aside specifically for spiritual practice are *formal practice sessions*. Your spiritual practice routine should also include *informal practice* interspersed in your daily life. Informal practice can help you maintain momentum between formal practice sessions.

Make time for an occasional *retreat*—an extended period of time reserved for spiritual practice. You don't have to leave home to do a retreat. Rest is an important part of a retreat; when you find yourself feeling fatigued, it's time to take a break. Solo retreats are more intense than retreats with others. Don't jump into an intensive, multi-day meditation retreat without having had much experience with meditation.

CHAPTER 4

ADJUST YOUR PRACTICE ROUTINE

CULTIVATING AWAKENING is like growing a garden; both projects require effort on your part, but neither project is fully under your control. You can't force awakening to happen any more than you can force a seed to sprout. All you can do is create conditions conducive to growth, observe what happens, make educated guesses about the causes of any problems, and make adjustments to correct for them.

Because of this, creating a spiritual practice routine isn't a one-off task; it's important to periodically assess your routine and adjust it (when necessary) to meet your changing needs. If you don't seem to be making progress in your practices and you feel like you're stuck, you probably are! It may be time to try something different. This chapter describes some general principles and strategies for assessing and adjusting your practice routine.

BALANCING YOUR PRACTICES

This book focuses on mindfulness and insight. There are other important aspects of awakening that aren't addressed in this book (such as compassion). Which facets of awakening should you focus on? That's up to you, but in general, I suggest you focus on the facets you're drawn toward. If you're drawn toward working on several, that's fine. What you're drawn toward will shift over time; go where you feel drawn. That's even true within a single session of formal practice; it's okay to shift practices mid-session.

If you're feeling stuck, one thing you can try is shifting your focus to a different facet of awakening. Different aspects of human development tend to be interrelated and mutually reinforcing, so if you feel stuck in relation to one facet of awakening, it's possible that a weakness in another one may be holding you back; developing more strength in that facet may lead to a breakthrough in the first. Early in my spiritual journey, I was very attracted to insight. However, I found that the work I did to develop vitality, mindfulness, and compassion was helpful (if not crucial) for making progress in insight.

WORKING YOUR EDGES

For each facet of awakening, you have several edges for growth. (For instance, vitality includes physical well-being, emotional well-being, and more.) The most effective way to awaken is to *work your edges;* you're working your edges when your practices feel challenging, but not overwhelming. Different spiritual practices help you work different edges.

Within each facet of awakening, your *degree* of awakening fluctuates over time—which means that the location of each of your edges keeps shifting. Awakening isn't a linear process like climbing straight to the top of a smooth-sided mountain; it's more like wandering over a vast landscape with many ups and downs. You'll have good days and bad days. Even a single formal practice session can include a number of ups and downs.

Just as different practices exercise different facets of awakening, different practices are appropriate for different states of mind. It's up to you to monitor your state of mind (and your skill level) and choose practices that are appropriate. If you choose practices that are too advanced, they'll seem too difficult and you won't get anywhere. If you choose practices that are too basic, they'll seem too easy and you won't be working your edges. Either way, your experience is likely to be one of boredom and/or frustration.

I believe effective spiritual practice is rarely, if ever, boring. When you're doing the appropriate practices for your state of mind, your practices will seem challenging yet do-able. You'll find your practices engaging, and you'll periodically have the satisfaction of recognizing you've made some progress in cultivating awakening.

MOTIVATING YOURSELF

Sometimes, when my attention has gotten wrapped up in other aspects of living, I've unintentionally put my spiritual practices on autopilot. When this happens, one way to light a fire under your practice routine is to contemplate your impending death. As Buddhist teacher Ken McLeod has pointed out, we can all be fairly certain we're going to die, and none of us knows exactly when this is going to happen. What happens *after* we die is even more of a mystery than what's happening right now. There's something about contemplating death that can really focus the mind on what's most important in life. Awaken while you can!

Other times, my practices have gotten stuck due to spiritual arrogance; I've gotten complacent about awakening because I've assumed I've reached the spiritual summit and there's nowhere (of any significance) left to go. This is a sad state of affairs, and a difficult dead end to escape from. Certainty that you've reached the spiritual summit is a symptom that you're embedded in a particular frame of reference. The best antidote to this is insight practice, which can help you disembed yourself from *all* frames of reference. (I discuss frames of reference and insight practice in part 3, "Cultivate Insight.") After letting go of the idea that there's an ultimate frame of reference, it becomes clear that there's no ultimate summit of awakening, either. I find this both humbling and exciting. As I see it, the journey of awakening has no endpoint. That means there's always more to explore—and *that's* something I can get excited about.

SEEKING GUIDANCE

When you haven't been able to resolve a stuck point on your own, the most efficient thing to do is often to seek guidance from a trusted spiritual mentor or teacher—or, better yet, several! Your mentors and teachers can point out stuck points in your practice that you may not even be aware of. You should feel less confused—not more—after a discussion with a spiritual teacher; if you feel more confused, look elsewhere for guidance. I've sometimes found it helpful to work with several teachers and mentors concurrently to get a variety of perspectives on my practice.

SUMMARY

Periodically assess your spiritual practice routine and adjust it to meet your changing needs. If you don't seem to be making progress in your practices and you feel like you're stuck, it may be time to try something different.

Focus on the facets of awakening that you're drawn toward. If you're feeling stuck, try shifting your focus.

Different practices are appropriate for different states of mind; monitor your state of mind (and your skill level) and choose practices that are appropriate. When you're doing the appropriate practices, your practices will seem challenging yet do-able.

When you've put your spiritual practices on auto-pilot, contemplating your death can refocus your mind on what's most important in life. You may get complacent about awakening when you assume you've reached the spiritual summit and there's nowhere (of any significance) left to go; however, as I see it, the journey of awakening has no endpoint.

When you haven't been able to resolve a stuck point on your own, seek guidance from a trusted spiritual mentor or teacher. I've sometimes found it helpful to work with several teachers and mentors concurrently to get a variety of perspectives on my practice.

❦

So far, in part 1, you've developed a spiritual practice routine and learned the basics of meditation. Next, in part 2, you'll deepen your meditation skills, learning how to use concentration and other meditation practices to cultivate mindfulness (a stable, clear, expansive awareness of a wide range of your current experiences). (Mindfulness is a prerequisite for cultivating insight, which is explored in part 3.)

PART TWO

CULTIVATE
MINDFULNESS

CHAPTER 5

RECOGNIZE YOUR THINKING HABIT

THINKING is an important, useful skill that helps us make sense of life. Unfortunately, thinking can also be an involuntary habit that can be problematic in a number of ways. In this chapter, I explore the nature of involuntary thinking and the problems it can cause.

TWO FLAVORS OF SUBJECTIVE EXPERIENCE

Let's start by defining some terms. A *subjective experience* or *experience* is what happens when you're aware of anything. (For instance, when I look out my window, I have an experience of a tree. When I attend to my feeling state right now, I have an experience of tiredness.) We can define two flavors of experience: *conceptual experiences* involve concepts; *nonconceptual experiences* don't. For instance, when you see an elephant and the word *elephant* comes to mind, this is a conceptual experience (because it involves the concept *elephant*.) Likewise, when you hear the word *elephant* and an elephant comes to mind, this is also a conceptual experience. However, when you look at (or imagine) an elephant and simply notice its visual appearance—without putting words to that appearance—you're having a nonconceptual experience.

To determine the degree to which an experience is conceptual, ask yourself, "How hard would it be to communicate this experience in words?" Conceptual experiences tend to be easier to put into words because of the close relationship between concepts and language; nonconceptual experiences tend to be more difficult to put into words.

For instance, I were to put my current thoughts into words, I might quickly and concisely say, "It might be nice to have lunch soon." If I were to try to put the totality of what I'm hearing into words, I might have a harder time. I could say, "I'm hearing wind in the trees and some other sounds I can't quite identify." I might try to describe those other sounds; I could go on and on for quite a while, and I *still* might not feel that I had adequately described the totality of what I'm hearing.

Most experiences have both conceptual and nonconceptual aspects. For instance, if I look at a chair, my experience of the chair includes both nonconceptual aspects (the visual *image* of the chair, my feelings about the chair, and so forth) and conceptual aspects (*knowing* it's a chair, knowing what I can *do* with chairs, and so forth). When I pay more attention to the nonconceptual aspects, I'm more aware of the chair on a sensory, feeling level. When I pay more attention to the conceptual aspects, I'm more aware of the chair on a practical level.

IN OTHER FRAMEWORKS

Subjective experience seems related to the philosophical and psychological concept of *qualia*.

The Experience of Thinking

Now, let's turn our attention to the experience of thinking. To better understand this experience, let's consider an extreme case of thinking: being lost in thought. What's that experience like? This is tricky to investigate because as soon as you start paying attention to the experience you're *having* when you're lost in thought, you're no longer lost in thought! Perhaps the best we can do is the following: as soon as we notice we've been lost in thought, we can immediately recall what we've been experiencing in the moments just before. I suggest you set an intention to try this and see what you discover.

I find that when I'm lost in thought, I'm a bit zombie-like. I might be wandering around the house or driving my car, but I'm on autopilot—I'm only somewhat aware of what's going on around me. I'm generally not aware that I'm thinking. Mostly, what I'm aware of are the things I'm thinking *about*. It's as if I'm living in another world—a world of conceptual experience.

What happens to the world of *nonconceptual* experiences when we're lost in thought? (For instance, what happens to sounds, smells, tastes, visual images, tactile sensations, and feelings)? These experiences get neglected; little or no attention is available for them since most of our attention is wrapped up in thinking. We don't necessarily stop *having* nonconceptual experiences; however, we have a reduced *awareness* of them. In summary, when we're lost in thought, we lose touch with *an entire realm of experience*—the realm of nonconceptual experience.

⁂

Being lost in thought is an extreme form of something that most of us experience frequently, if not constantly: involuntary thinking. We tend to consider thinking to be a voluntary process, but that's not quite accurate. In my experience, I have some ability to steer the *course* of my thinking—but I have much less ability to choose *whether* I think. (If you don't believe thinking is involuntary, set a timer for 60 seconds and don't allow yourself to have a single thought until the timer goes off. Good luck!)

Thinking can be not only involuntary, but also somewhat unconscious, in the following sense: when we're thinking, we may be aware of what we're thinking about, but we're often unaware *that* we're thinking or that there's any *alternative* to thinking. We're caught in an involuntary process that we're not even aware of. (Once we become *aware* that we're thinking, our thinking process is no longer unconscious, and we have an opportunity to redirect our attention toward other activities.)

IN OTHER FRAMEWORKS

Involuntary thinking seems related to the concept of *automatic thoughts* in cognitive behavioral therapy.

PROBLEMS CAUSED BY THINKING

I'm a big fan of thinking. I find it to be a useful faculty that allows me to make sense of my life, anticipate future events, and make plans. I wouldn't want to completely give up thinking—and I think you should be suspicious of any spiritual path that suggests you should.

However, I also believe that most of us (myself included) have a thinking *habit*. Those of us who are intellectually inclined (like me) may have a stronger thinking habit than others. This habit can create some problems for us.

REDUCED AWARENESS OF NONCONCEPTUAL EXPERIENCES

As I noted above, when you're thinking, you have less attention available for nonconceptual experiences. One effect of this is that sensory experiences become less vivid. In my thirties, I started noticing that my sensory experiences seemed a lot less vivid than they had been when I was younger; I found this disturbing. When I started meditating, vividness started returning to my sensory experiences.

Here's a related issue: those of us who are frequently lost in thought tend to have challenges with intimate relationships. That's because intimacy requires empathy, and empathy requires access to our feelings; our feelings are nonconceptual experiences that can be difficult to access when our attention is wrapped up in thinking.

REDUCED ACCESS TO NON-RATIONAL WAYS OF KNOWING

When we're lost in thought, we lose access to *other ways* of making sense of life that can be beneficial *complements* to thinking. Thinking has its benefits: it can be precise and methodical. However, it's also relatively slow compared to other faculties like intuition.

Intuition is like an analog computer or a neural network that can quickly analyze large amounts of information. I use both thinking and intuition to find my way in life; I find them both valuable.

CONCEPTUAL RIGIDITY

Thinking is a conceptual activity that involves (and requires) a conceptual framework—a conceptual model of whatever it is that we're thinking about. It seems to me that thinking energizes and stabilizes these frameworks, making it more difficult for us to escape their limitations. (Every framework has limitations since any conceptual model casts light on some aspects of what's being modeled and obscures other aspects.)

When you've been thinking about a problem for a while and you feel stuck, what's the best thing to do? Stop thinking about it! Go for a walk, take a shower, sleep on it, and so forth. When you stop thinking about it, you stop energizing the conceptual frame of reference that's been limiting your thinking. Often, when you return to the problem, you can see it with a fresh perspective because your frame of reference has become more malleable.

When we're thinking involuntarily and unconsciously, we don't have the option to take a break from what we're thinking about. Our familiar frames of reference are constantly being energized and stabilized. The more we're lost in thought, the more rigid our frames of reference become.

DIFFICULTY CULTIVATING INSIGHT

Insight practice is described in part 3, "Cultivate Insight;" it's the experiential exploration of the relationships between self, reality, awareness, and subjective experience. If you're interested in cultivating insight, note that too much unconscious, involuntary thinking makes the more advanced levels of insight (level 4 and beyond) much harder to cultivate—thus my emphasis on cultivating mindfulness for those seeking insight. (Mindfulness is introduced in the following chapter.)

In my own journey, I initially had little interest in cultivating mindfulness; I wanted to get to cultivating insight as quickly as possible. However, at the urging of my mentors, I ended up spending a significant amount of time and energy cultivating mindfulness; now I understand the wisdom in this and I've developed a great appreciation of mindfulness for its own sake, as well.

SUMMARY

A *subjective experience* or *experience* is what happens when you're aware of anything. We can define two flavors of experience: a *conceptual experience* involves concepts; a *nonconceptual experience* doesn't. To determine the degree to which an experience is conceptual, ask yourself, "How hard would it be to communicate this experience in words?"

Thinking can be both involuntary and somewhat unconscious; when we're thinking, we may be aware of what were thinking about, but we're often unaware *that* we're thinking or that there's any *alternative* to thinking.

Most of us have a thinking *habit* that can be problematic in several ways: thinking leaves less attention available for nonconceptual experiences, decreases access to other ways of making sense of life (such as intuition), and makes it harder for us to escape our familiar frames of reference. In addition, too much unconscious, involuntary thinking makes it much harder to cultivate advanced levels of insight.

Chapter 6

Understand Mindfulness and Concentration

G IVEN THE VARIOUS PROBLEMS caused by involuntary thinking (that we identified in the previous chapter), I suggest you start transforming your relationship with thinking; I suggest you learn to make thinking more a conscious choice and less an unconscious habit. How might you do this? In involuntary thinking, your attention is unconsciously and involuntarily diverted into thinking; to prevent this from happening, you must learn to *recognize* where your attention is at and *direct it* where you want it to be. This is the essence of cultivating mindfulness through the practice of concentration. This chapter defines *mindfulness* and *concentration;* the following chapters describe practices for *cultivating* mindfulness (through concentration and other practices).

Your Field of Subjective Experience

A clear definition of mindfulness will be helpful for our discussion. Let's call the set of all your current subjective experiences your *field of experience*. (This is actually more like a field or a space than a set since experiences aren't distinct units with clear boundaries.) Then we can concisely define *mindfulness* as awareness of your field of experience. Equivalently, it's awareness of your current experiences. (I expand this preliminary definition later in this chapter.)

But, aren't we *always* aware of our current experiences? Not exactly. We tend to have a fairly simplistic, binary view of awareness —we tend to believe we're either aware of something or we're not. The same is true of attention—we tend to think of our attention as either being "on" an experience or not. For cultivating mindfulness, it will be helpful to have a more nuanced understanding of awareness and attention.

Your *attention* is the mental faculty that supports selective awareness of your experiences; your *awareness* of an experience is the degree to which you perceive it. Think of your field of experience as a vast landscape of experiences, and your attention as light shining on that landscape. At any given time, depending on what the light is doing, some parts of that landscape will be well lit, others will be dimly lit, and others will be in shadows. Likewise, at any given time, depending on what your attention is doing, you'll have a clear awareness of some of your experiences, you'll have less awareness of others, and you'll hardly be aware of other experiences at all. Your attentional *field of view* is the portion of your field of experience that you currently have a clear awareness of.

FOUR ASPECTS OF ATTENTION

Since mindfulness is awareness of your current experiences and attention is the faculty that *supports* that awareness, your level of mindfulness is directly related to the quality of your attention. The quality of your attention is a function of (at least) four *aspects of attention*: stability, clarity, expansiveness, and range. (Most spiritual practices for cultivating mindfulness work by strengthening one or more of these aspects of attention.) Below, I define these four aspects, illustrating them with the "light on a landscape" metaphor that I introduced in the section above.

- The *stability* of your attention is your capacity to pay attention to what you choose to, without getting distracted. (If attention were light, stability would be your ability to direct that light.) Without stability, your attention is easily diverted into involuntary thinking.
- The *clarity* of your attention is your ability to bring vivid, continuous awareness to your experiences. (If attention were light, clarity would be the intensity and continuity of that light.) (B. Alan Wallace's work has informed my concepts of *stability* and *clarity* of attention.)
- The *expansiveness* of your attention is your ability to expand your attentional field of view to attend to many experiences simultaneously. (If attention were a beam of light, expansiveness would be your ability to widen that beam.)
- The *range* of your attention is your ability to attend to a diversity of experiences. For instance, if you find thinking easy but noticing feelings difficult, your attentional range would be weighted toward thoughts and away from feelings. (If attention were light and your experiences were spread across a landscape, your attentional range would correspond to the portion of the landscape that you're able to light up. In *your* landscape of experience, what areas are well lit and what areas are in relative darkness?)

DEFINING MINDFULNESS

Having defined these four aspects of attention, we can define four corresponding aspects of awareness: *stability, clarity, expansiveness,* and *range* of awareness are what you get when you have stability, clarity, expansiveness, and range of attention (respectively). Then we can restate our definition of mindfulness more precisely: *mindfulness* is a stable, clear, expansive awareness of a wide range of one's current experiences.

Mindfulness is much more than an antidote to unconscious, involuntary thinking; it's a foundational skill for cultivating insight and other facets of awakening. When I was at the beginning of my spiritual journey—with most of my attention wrapped up in unconscious, involuntary thinking most of the time—I had a hard time understanding or imagining many of the experiences reported by those farther along than me. At one point, I saw a drawing that metaphorically represented the experience of awakening. The drawing depicted a man climbing through some kind of threshold and discovering a new world. I desperately wanted to be that man, and I wondered if I ever would. I eventually discovered that cultivating mindfulness is the first step in climbing through that threshold.

IN OTHER FRAMEWORKS

I should note that in other frameworks—such as psychology and Buddhism—I've seen the term *mindfulness* used in a variety of ways, some of which differ from my usage. In general, I've seen the term *mindfulness* used in two ways: in the first usage, mindfulness refers to an awareness of one's current experiences; in the second usage, mindfulness refers to an awareness of one's current experiences *plus an evaluation of those experiences* in terms of a particular framework for awakening. The first usage seems to show up more often in psychology; the second usage seems to show up more often in Buddhism.

I've chosen to make my definition of mindfulness consistent with the first usage; my definition of *mindfulness* requires only *awareness* of experience—not *conceptual understanding* of experience. (My definition of *mindfulness* doesn't even require understanding one's experience as *experience* or as *subjective.*) It may seem that *mindfulness,* as I've defined it, is synonymous with *awareness*—but this isn't the case; my precise definition of *mindfulness* is a *stable, clear, expansive* awareness of a *wide range* of one's current experiences.

There are two reasons why I've defined *mindfulness* in this way. First, I want to avoid making my definition of *mindfulness* dependent on any particular conceptual framework (other than the minimal framework related to *experience, awareness,* and *attention,* as I've defined them). This is consistent with my view that there's no ultimate framework for awakening (a view that I describe in the section "Level 7: No Reference" in chapter 14). Second, I appreciate how distinguishing *mindfulness* and *conceptual understanding* (as opposed to conflating these concepts) gives us a more fine-grained lexicon that allows us to distinguish awareness of an experience from a conceptual understanding of that experience.

In cases where we want to speak more specifically about mindfulness in relation to a particular concept or framework, we can indicate this by adding additional qualifiers to the term *mindfulness.* For instance, we might say *mindfulness of emotion* to refer to a recognition of experiences of emotion, with a clear, expansive awareness of a wide range of those experiences. Similarly, we might say *mindfulness with moral discernment* to refer to a clear, expansive awareness of a wide range of one's current experiences, plus a conceptual understanding of those experiences in relation to a particular moral framework.

DEFINING CONCENTRATION

I use the term *concentration* to refer to a practice in which you intentionally direct and clarify your attention in order to cultivate attentional stability and clarity. (This practice is described in detail in the following chapters.) I also use the term *concentration* to refer to the spectrum of states of mind that result from this practice—states of mind characterized by increasingly stable, clear awareness.

Since stability and clarity are two of the four aspects of attention that support mindfulness, concentration practices are an excellent way to cultivate mindfulness. You can also integrate practices for increasing the expansiveness and range of your attention into your concentration practices; this can help you cultivate mindfulness even more effectively.

⁂

I'm ambivalent about the term *concentration*. To me, the term *concentration* connotes effort. Concentration does require effort—at first. However, the effort that's required is a *relaxed* effort—and surprisingly, as you progress to increasingly advanced stages of concentration, less and less effort is involved, and the practice becomes increasingly pleasant. Think about it like this: at first, the practice of concentration requires you to *concentrate* as you build the strength of your attention; through this effort, your attention becomes more *concentrated* (like a concentrated beam of light) and less effort is required to practice.

The other issue I have with the term *concentration* is that it makes me think of focusing on something *very small*. The term *single-pointed attention,* which has been used to characterize advanced stages of concentration, shares this same issue. Concentration is characterized by *stable, clear* attention—not *limited expansiveness* of attention. It's possible to cultivate concentration using very expansive objects of attention—and, in fact, doing so can support mindfulness more effectively.

Despite the above reservations, I choose to use the term *concentration* because it's commonly used in Buddhism to refer to similar practices and states of mind.

SUMMARY

Let's call the set of all your current subjective experiences your *field of experience.* Then we can concisely define *mindfulness* as awareness of your field of experience or awareness of your current experiences. Your *attention* is the mental faculty that supports selective awareness of your experiences; your *awareness* of an experience is the degree to which you perceive it. Your attentional *field of view* is the portion of your field of experience that you currently have a clear awareness of.

The quality of your attention is a function of (at least) four aspects of attention: stability, clarity, expansiveness, and range. The *stability* of your attention is your capacity to pay attention to what you choose to, without getting distracted. The *clarity* of your attention is your ability to bring vivid, continuous awareness to your experiences. The *expansiveness* of your attention is your ability to expand your attentional field of view to attend to many experiences simultaneously. The *range* of your attention is your ability to attend to a diversity of experiences. *Stability, clarity, expansiveness,* and *range of awareness* are what you get when you have stability, clarity, expansiveness, and range of attention (respectively). Having defined the above terms, we can now define *mindfulness* more precisely as a stable, clear, expansive awareness of a wide range of one's current experiences. (In other frameworks—such as psychology and Buddhism—I've seen the term mindfulness used in a variety of ways, some of which differ from my usage.)

To prevent involuntary thinking, you must learn to recognize where your attention is at and direct it where you want it to be. This is the essence of cultivating mindfulness through the practice of concentration. I use the term *concentration* to refer to a practice in which you intentionally direct and clarify your attention in order to cultivate attentional stability and clarity; I also use the term *concentration* to refer to the spectrum of states of mind that result from this practice—states of mind characterized by increasingly stable, clear awareness. Concentration practices are an excellent way to cultivate mindfulness, and mindfulness is a foundational skill for cultivating insight and other facets of awakening.

CHAPTER 7

OVERCOME COMPLETE DISTRACTION

I N THE REMAINDER of part 2, I provide instructions for cultivating mindfulness via the practice of concentration. I describe a series of nine milestones that can guide you from complete distraction through beginning, intermediate, and advanced levels of concentration. I've been working with this approach for a number of years in my own practice routine, and I've found it to be quite effective.

(Besides being informed by personal experience, my views on cultivating concentration have also been informed by B. Alan Wallace's book *The Attention Revolution* and by section 1—"Establishing Concentration through Mindfulness with Breathing"—of Shaila Catherine's book *Wisdom Wide and Deep*. I've found each of these books to be helpful, and I recommend them. However, the views expressed in this book are my own; they are not intended to represent the views of any other persons, traditions, religions, lineages, organizations, or professions that I may be associated with.)

THE BEGINNING CONCENTRATION MILESTONES

In this approach to concentration practice, you traverse a series of nine *concentration milestones:* four beginning milestones, three intermediate milestones, and two advanced milestones. As you traverse them, your state of mind shifts as your attention becomes increasingly stable and clear. It would be nice if we could just traverse these milestones once (and be done with it), but my experience has been that I usually start over at the first milestone with each new meditation session. However, with practice, I've learned to traverse these milestones more quickly.

The *beginning concentration milestones* are focused on building attentional stability. As you traverse them, you gradually address the problem of *complete distraction*, in which your attention gets completely drawn away from your *chosen object of attention* (that is, whatever you've been intending to pay attention to) and you completely forget this chosen object for a while. The following are the beginning milestones:

- **1st milestone:** You can attend to your chosen object for a few seconds at a time; after that, you get completely distracted.
- **2nd milestone:** You can attend to your chosen object for a minute at a time; after that, you get completely distracted.
- **3rd milestone:** Your attention is on your chosen object most of the time; however, you still have occasional, brief periods of complete distraction.
- **4th milestone:** You avoid complete distraction; however, you still get partially distracted, and your chosen object completely fades out occasionally.

Complete distraction is a significant problem, because when you're completely distracted, you lose the ability to do *any* spiritual practice (consciously, anyway); that's why complete distraction is the first problem to address in concentration practice. The best way to start addressing it is through a daily meditation practice (as described in chapter 2).

In your meditation sessions, choose an object of attention and attempt to rest your attention on that object. Eventually, you'll notice that you're completely distracted—probably lost in thought—and your attention is no longer on your chosen object. At this point, return your attention to your chosen object and—once again—attempt to rest it there. Each time you notice that you're distracted and return your attention to your chosen object, you get a bit better at noticing distraction, and your attention becomes a bit more stable.

CHOOSING AN OBJECT OF ATTENTION

Some objects of attention are easier to focus on than others. Unvarying, narrowly defined objects tend to be easier to work with than those that are more subtle, variable, or expansive. The key to making progress in traversing the beginning milestones is to choose an object that's challenging enough but not too challenging, so you're constantly working your edges.

I recommend the breath as an object of attention for traversing the beginning milestones—if it works for you. However, for many beginners, the breath may be too subtle and variable to focus on easily. If that's the case for you, try placing a small physical item in front of you—something you enjoy looking at—and use the visual image of that item as your chosen object. (When I was first getting started with concentration meditation, I used this type of visual object for quite a while, and it worked well for me.) You may notice that your eyes make subtle jerky movements; try to relax your eyes, and let your gaze be as stable as possible.

The only problem with this type of visual object is that it's so unvarying that it doesn't exercise the clarity of your attention much —so, once you've mastered the beginning milestones using a visual object, try switching to the breath and traversing these milestones again. Taking a few deep breaths when you start a session of meditation can help you loosen up your breathing—but after that, don't force your breath to do anything special; just let it do its thing, and rest your attention on it in a relaxed way. Notice the wave-like nature of your breathing. Imagine you're sitting by the ocean, watching the waves roll in. Your eyes can be open, closed, or half open; it's up to you. (I usually just let my eyelids do what they want to do.)

MEASURING CONCENTRATION

The beginning, intermediate, and advanced concentration milestones can be thought of as a measure of concentration (meaning a system for measuring concentration). You can work with this system to help you focus your effort as you cultivate higher levels of concentration.

In a given meditation session, the most basic way to work with the milestones is to make it your first goal to attain the first milestone's criteria; then, start measuring your level of concentration and start working your way up the milestones. Alternatively, you can start your session by using the milestones to measure your current level of concentration; then choose your first goal accordingly. (If you're currently at the third milestone, your first goal would be to reach the fourth). If you're feeling ambitious, you can even choose an intermediate or advanced milestone as your first goal, right from the start of your session (without measuring your level of concentration first).

Over the course of your session, you may discover that your level of concentration has dropped; when this happens, adjust your goal accordingly. Don't expect a steady upward climb; you can expect your path through the milestones to go up and down like a roller coaster.

Starting with the third milestone, there's an important aspect of this measure of concentration that I've intentionally left unspecified and implicit: the duration over which the milestone's criteria are to be met. For instance, consider the fourth milestone's criteria: "you avoid complete distraction." You should read this as "you avoid complete distraction *for x seconds/minutes/hours.*"

I haven't specified the duration criteria (x) for these milestones because I believe that for the most part, these criteria are arbitrary. That's not to say they're not important; obviously, the longer you can maintain a state, the more robust it is. (There's a big difference between avoiding complete distraction for five *seconds* versus five *hours!*)

I suggest you choose your own duration criteria and tune these criteria to the type of practice you're doing. For a thirty-minute to sixty-minute daily meditation session (outside of a retreat context), you might choose duration criteria of somewhere between two and ten minutes for each milestone. In a retreat context, you might raise the bar by choosing longer duration criteria—anywhere from twenty minutes to several hours. If you choose shorter duration criteria, you optimize your practice for shorter periods of *higher levels* of concentration; if you want to optimize for longer periods of *more stable states* of concentration, choose longer duration criteria.

(In other approaches to awakening that I've seen, duration criteria have been specified on the long end of the scale—from thirty minutes to several hours. While this may be ideal for cultivating stable states of concentration in a retreat context, it seems to me that measuring concentration this way isn't as useful or appropriate *outside of* a retreat context. I view daily practice sessions as more like sprinting than like running a marathon. Would you measure your sprinting speed over the course of a two-hour run? Of course not, because that wouldn't be a sprint.)

With practice, you can learn to estimate which milestone you're at without having to actually wait out the duration x. Of course, waiting out the duration and observing what happens will give you a more accurate measure of your level of concentration; however, I believe there's also value in tracking a more fine-grained estimate of which milestone you're currently at.

TRAVERSING THE BEGINNING MILESTONES

If you're using the breath as your chosen object, to get to the first milestone, use the sensations of breathing throughout your body; then, to get to the second milestone, use the sensations of breathing in your abdomen. You can experiment with counting your breaths at the start of each inhalation, to see if that helps. Make each count brief, so that most of your attention stays on the sensations of breathing; the counting is just a reminder to keep your attention on the breath. Start your count at "one;" after you get to "eight," start over again at "one." (If you end up at a number higher than "eight," this means you've gotten distracted; start over again at "one.")

If you want, you can experiment with using a stopwatch to track how long you can keep your attention on your chosen object before you get completely distracted. Start the stopwatch, then rest your attention on your chosen object. Stop the stopwatch when you notice that you're completely distracted, and use the elapsed time to estimate how long you were able to rest your attention on the object before you got distracted. (When you reach the second milestone, stop using a stopwatch, because manipulating the stopwatch will become too much of a distraction.)

If you're using the breath as your chosen object, to get to the third and fourth milestones, use the sensations of breathing around your upper lip and nostrils. Notice the sensations there, even between breaths, and even when the breath is shallow or when it has stopped. If you've been counting breaths, start weaning yourself off of counting when you get to the third milestone; by the time you reach the fourth milestone, you shouldn't be counting breaths anymore.

You'll notice that as you traverse these milestones, your breathing tends to slow down and become more subtle. As it does, the sensations associated with breathing become more subtle and more challenging to attend to. This is actually a good thing because attending to these subtle sensations helps build your attentional stability and clarity.

To avoid getting distracted as you work with subtle objects of attention, you'll need to make your chosen object more engaging by intentionally experiencing it more vividly. (This becomes important as you attempt to reach the third milestone and beyond.) Raise the level of energy going into your attention by taking more interest in your experience of the object. Pay more attention to it—but not so much that you lose relaxation or attentional stability. As the object becomes more vivid and engaging, it gets easier to rest your attention on it without getting distracted. This is also a way to address *attentional dullness* (meaning lack of attentional clarity). (Attentional dullness is described in greater detail below.)

⤞❧⤝

When you get to the fourth milestone, you've (temporarily) overcome complete distraction—meaning that you can avoid complete distraction for an arbitrary time duration of your choosing; let's say ten minutes. (I address the issue of what time duration to choose in the section "Measuring Concentration," above.)

Despite overcoming complete distraction, problems still remain. For one thing, you still get *partially* distracted; *partial distraction* occurs when something distracts you from your chosen object and most of your attention shifts to what's distracting you—but your attention never *completely* leaves your chosen object. (So you end up with *most* of your attention on what's distracting you and *some* of your attention on your chosen object.)

At the fourth milestone, your mastery of complete distraction makes another issue more evident: when you're attending to your chosen object, if you look closely, you'll notice that your awareness of it isn't as vivid as it could be, and, in addition, your awareness of it fades in and out—occasionally fading out completely. (The experience itself doesn't change; you just lose awareness of the experience.) The *fade-out* may last anywhere from a fraction of a second to several seconds or more.

Lack of vividness and fade-outs are due to *dullness* (meaning lack of attentional clarity); when there's insufficient energy in your attention, your awareness of your chosen object simply fades out of awareness. (In *complete dullness,* your awareness of your chosen object periodically fades out completely.) If your attention were a beam of light, dullness would be a condition where the light source has insufficient power and periodically grows dimmer. (This is different from distraction, in which the beam shifts direction to illuminate something other than your chosen object.) To counteract dullness, raise the level of energy going into your attention (as described earlier in this section).

USING INTROSPECTION AND NOTING

As I noted in chapter 5, before we start cultivating mindfulness, thinking is mostly an unconscious, involuntary process. (Of course, we're generally conscious of what we're thinking *about*—but we're generally *unconscious* of the *fact* that we're thinking.) The unconscious, involuntary nature of thinking becomes quite obvious as soon as you start practicing concentration meditation. You rest your attention on your chosen object—everything seems to be going fine—then, all of a sudden, you notice that you've been lost in thought, having totally forgotten your chosen object. This happens again and again.

When you notice that you've been lost in thought, you've exercised a capacity called *introspection,* which allows you to examine or scrutinize what's going on in your mind. Introspection is how you make unconscious mental processes conscious; it increases your level of mindfulness by expanding the range of your attention and awareness to include these mental processes.

Think of introspection as quality control for your meditation practice. Rather than just waiting to notice that you've been lost in thought, learn to engage introspection intentionally and continuously as you meditate. This means most of your attention will be on your chosen object, but some of your attention will be reserved for gently but vigilantly scrutinizing what your intellect and attention are up to. You can think of this as taking your attention itself as a secondary object of attention. See if you can notice what it *feels like* the moment your attention starts to waver.

There are at least two approaches to introspection: *diagnosis* (in which you look for specific problems such as distraction and dullness) and *remembering the goal* (in which you remember or imagine the state of mind you want to be in and notice differences between your current state and this goal state). I recommend both approaches. Without diagnosis, it's easy to fool yourself into thinking you're further along than you actually are. Without remembering the goal, it's easy to get lost in diagnostic details. Diagnosis helps you move away from problems while remembering the goal helps you move toward where you want to be. Diagnosis leads to steady but incremental progress while remembering the goal leads to less dependable but (potentially) more significant leaps. (If you've experienced the goal state in the past, sometimes simply remembering the experience of *being* in that state is enough to actually put you *back* in that state. The more recently you've experienced that state, the more likely this is to work.)

Introspection becomes even more powerful when combined with a technique called *noting*, in which you name what you're trying to notice as soon as you notice it. This simple act of naming helps bring that phenomenon more solidly into consciousness and helps you recognize that phenomenon more easily the next time it shows up. Like introspection, noting increases your level of mindfulness by expanding the range of your attention and awareness.

You can use introspection and noting in both meditation and daily life to help you become more conscious of many types of phenomena. However, in mindfulness meditation, it's especially helpful to learn to recognize two things: distraction (when thinking or other phenomena are drawing your attention away from your chosen object) and dullness (when your experience is getting dull and losing vividness because your attention is insufficiently energized). When you notice distraction or dullness, you can silently think the words "distraction" or "dullness," respectively—or you can just make a mental note of the distraction or dullness without thinking the words.

⁓❦⁓

For me, getting to the fourth milestone (and beyond) often requires steadfast introspection and noting of both distraction and dullness. Without sufficient introspection, it's easy for me to hang out around the second and third milestones indefinitely, fooling myself into thinking I'm farther along than I actually am. What helps me be more honest with myself is to do an introspection spot check, asking myself how much thinking I've been doing in the last fifteen seconds. If I notice that I was lost in thought *at all* during that time, I can be sure I'm not at the fourth milestone yet.

EXPERIENCES YOU MAY HAVE

When you first start cultivating concentration, there's a hump to get over. Concentration practice starts getting dramatically more pleasant as you approach the intermediate milestones; until then, some perseverance and dedication are required. The following are some meditative experiences you may encounter as you traverse the beginning milestones.

SLEEPINESS

As I was starting to learn how to meditate, I found that as soon as my thoughts slowed down a bit, I'd fall asleep! This happened fairly consistently, whether or not I'd gotten enough sleep the night before. I guess my mind was so accustomed to thinking that when my thinking slowed down, my mind decided it was time to take a nap! Falling asleep is an extreme form of dullness (or lack of attentional clarity). I found that meditating with my eyes open and meditating when I was more awake were somewhat helpful antidotes to falling asleep, but the only thing that *really* helped was continued practice.

These days, when I start falling asleep while I'm meditating, it's usually because I didn't get enough sleep the night before. When I notice this happening, I'll usually take a break from meditation and take a nap.

BOREDOM

I haven't experienced much boredom while meditating. However, I know this is something that some people do struggle with—especially as they traverse the beginning milestones. If you find yourself bored while meditating, here are some suggestions that may help.

As you're paying attention to your chosen object, it may seem that there's nothing you need to do except wait until you get distracted; perhaps this is where the sense of boredom arises. If you make meditation a waiting game, it's not going to be very interesting—and you probably won't develop concentration as quickly as you could. There's *way* more to meditation than waiting. The antidote to boredom in meditation is to go beyond waiting and take interest in what you're doing. There are at least two ways to do that: you can take an interest in your chosen object (what you're attempting to rest your attention on) and you can take an interest in what your mind is up to. I recommend you do both.

Taking interest in your chosen object counteracts attentional dullness. *You chose* this object—now, *don't neglect it!* Examine your chosen object as closely as you can, as if you're experiencing it for the first time. Don't miss a single moment of this experience! Pump up the energy with which you're experiencing your object so that you experience it as vividly as possible. This is *your life* going by—don't miss it!

Taking interest in what your mind is up to counteracts distraction. *Don't let distraction surprise you.* It's really very predictable. You'll find that you get distracted on a regular basis. By noticing your *pattern* of distraction, you can learn to predict—*down to the second*—when you're going to get distracted. As that time approaches, use pay close attention to what your mind is up to! (By *your mind,* I mean your attention, thoughts, emotions, impulses, and more.) (Paying attention to what your mind is up to is the process of *introspection,* which is described in the following chapter.) What's the experience of impending distraction? Find out! Does distraction happen suddenly or gradually? Get curious about it. See if you can catch it sneaking up on you, and see if you can head it off!

As you take interest in what you're doing, meditation becomes dramatic and suspenseful; it's *anything but* boring. Can you fulfill your commitment to your chosen object, giving it your complete, undivided attention—or will you allow dullness and distraction to seduce you? Moment by moment, the question becomes, who's going to win—you or dullness and distraction?

FRUSTRATION

Meditation can be frustrating at times as you traverse the beginning milestones. Again and again, you find yourself lost in thought when you want to be attending to your chosen object instead. Meditation brings you face-to-face with your limited level of attentional stability and forces you to confront it. Unfortunately, I don't know any way around this process; you just have to go through it (like I did). What's called for is relaxed, consistent, steadfast effort. Remember, each time you notice that you're lost in thought, you've *already recovered* from distraction, and you've already made your concentration muscles a little bit stronger. If you find yourself getting too frustrated, take a break.

The process of building enough attentional stability to traverse the beginning milestones may take some time; possibly, a long time. It's hard for me to say exactly how long it took me because I wasn't working with this model of concentration in the early stages of my meditation practice; however, I estimate that it probably took years of daily practice. (It's quite possible that it would have taken less time if I'd had this model to guide me from the beginning.)

While a certain level of alertness and watchfulness is required for concentration, traversing the beginning milestones isn't a process you can power through via intense focus. (That didn't stop me from trying, though, and you may need to try this too as you experiment to find the right balance between relaxation and alertness. Once, I was meditating intensely while periodically working a stopwatch, and a friend commented, "I don't know what you're doing—but it's not meditation!") Too much intensity interferes with your ability to relax—and meditation requires a *relaxed* effort. If you don't relax your body and mind, your intellect will be overly activated and it will be harder to avoid getting lost in thought.

THE ENERGETIC ASPECT OF BREATHING

In physics, *energy* refers to the ability of a system to perform work. Around the third and fourth milestones, I often start noticing the sensations of a phenomenon that seems to be driving the work of breathing; I call this phenomenon the *energetic aspect of breathing*. These energetic sensations are distinct from the tactile sensations of breathing; the tactile sensations include the feeling of your muscles moving and the feeling of air moving against your skin, while the energetic sensations include more diffuse, wave-like sensations related to the urge (or impulse) to breathe in and out.

To sense the energetic aspect of breathing, breathe out—then wait. Eventually, I guarantee that you will notice an impulse to breathe in! Notice how the impulse to breathe in and out is distinct from the muscular movements of breathing, and notice how your muscular movements may actually be out of sync with this impulse. This impulse is the energetic aspect of breathing. *Without changing* the energetic aspect, try synchronizing your muscular movements of breathing to the energetic aspect and notice what happens.

Attending to the energetic aspect of breathing builds this energy; as this happens, you may notice that you spontaneously start to relax and breathe more deeply. Because of this, attending to the energetic aspect of breathing is not only a mindfulness practice (that builds your attentional range) but also a vitality practice. When you notice the energetic aspect of breathing during concentration meditation, I suggest you experiment with switching to it as your object of attention.

THE SIGN

Around the fourth milestone, many people (but not all) start noticing an unusual visual phenomenon that starts showing up in the visual field during meditation. It can appear whether your eyes are open or closed. I call this phenomenon the *sign*.

The sign looks different for different people. For me, it often shows up as a pulsating wave-like pattern of light and dark that pulsates about once every four seconds. As my attention stabilizes, the sign often stabilizes too, into a pattern of symmetrical, concentric rings that close in on themselves toward the center of my field of vision with each pulse. I often find the sign to be captivating, beautiful, and quite psychedelic-looking. It sometimes looks a lot like what I imagine a will-o'-the-wisp might look.

I didn't know anything about the sign when it first started showing up for me, so at first, it disturbed me a bit—but I soon relaxed as I realized that it didn't seem at all harmful. For me, the sign has always dissipated quickly at the end of my formal meditation sessions. Sometimes it shows up outside of formal meditation at times when I'm especially mindful.

The sign is a sign that you are making good progress in cultivating concentration! Not only that, but it makes a great object of attention; it's quite subtle and somewhat diffuse, so attending to it is a good exercise for developing attentional clarity and expansiveness. When it shows up, I'll often take it as my object of attention. (The sign may appear and disappear, so switch back to the breath if the sign dissipates, and don't worry about this too much.) Closing your eyes may help you see the sign more clearly, but it may also make you drowsy; open your eyes if you find that you need to be more awake.

SUMMARY

In this chapter and the remainder of part 2, I provide instructions for cultivating mindfulness via concentration; I describe a series of nine *concentration milestones* that can guide you from complete distraction through beginning, intermediate, and advanced levels of concentration. As you traverse these milestones, your attention becomes increasingly stable and clear.

The *beginning concentration milestones* are focused on building attentional stability. As you traverse them, you gradually address the problem of *complete distraction,* in which your attention gets completely drawn away from your *chosen object of attention* (that is, whatever you've been intending to pay attention to). Complete distraction is a significant problem because when you're completely distracted, you lose the ability to do any spiritual practice. The best way to start addressing complete distraction is through a daily meditation practice (as described in chapter 2).

I recommend the breath as an object of attention for traversing the beginning milestones—if it works for you. If it doesn't, try placing a small physical item in front of you—something you enjoy looking at—and use the visual image of that item as your chosen object.

When you get to the last of the beginning milestones, you've (temporarily) overcome complete distraction. Despite overcoming complete distraction, problems still remain. For one thing, you still get partially distracted; *partial distraction* occurs when something distracts you from your chosen object and most of your attention shifts to what's distracting you—but your attention never completely leaves your chosen object.

Also, when you're attending to your chosen object, if you look closely, you'll notice that your awareness of it isn't as vivid as it could be, and, in addition, your awareness of it fades in and out—occasionally fading out completely. (The experience itself doesn't change; you just lose awareness of the experience.) The *fade-out* may last anywhere from a fraction of a second to several seconds or more.

Lack of vividness and fade-outs are due to *dullness* (meaning lack of attentional clarity); when there's insufficient energy in your attention, your awareness of your chosen object simply fades out of awareness. (In *complete dullness,* your awareness of your chosen object periodically fades out completely.) To counteract dullness, raise the level of energy going into your attention.

The capacity to examine or scrutinize what's going on in your mind is called *introspection*. Think of introspection as quality control for your meditation practice; learn to engage introspection intentionally and continuously as you meditate. Two approaches to introspection are *diagnosis* (in which you look for specific problems such as distraction and dullness) and *remembering the goal* (in which you remember or imagine the state of mind you want to be in and notice differences between your current state and this goal state). Introspection becomes even more powerful when combined with a technique called *noting*, in which you name what you're trying to notice as soon as you notice it. You can use introspection and noting in both meditation and daily life to help you become more conscious of many types of phenomena. However, in mindfulness meditation, it's especially helpful to learn to recognize two things: distraction and dullness.

Concentration practice starts getting dramatically more pleasant as you approach the intermediate milestones; until then, some perseverance and dedication are required. Some meditative experiences you may encounter as you traverse the beginning milestones include sleepiness, boredom, frustration, and the energetic aspect of breathing.

Around the last of the beginning milestones, many people (but not all) notice an unusual visual phenomenon that starts showing up in the visual field during meditation. It can appear whether your eyes are open or closed. I call this phenomenon the *sign*. The sign is a sign that you are making good progress in cultivating concentration! Not only that, but it makes a great object of attention.

Chapter 8

Overcome Partial Distraction and Dullness

To Get From the fourth milestone (the last beginning milestone) to the fifth milestone (the first intermediate milestone), you must raise your level of attentional clarity. You can do this through introspection, noticing (and noting) dullness, and paying more attention to your chosen object (as described in the previous chapter).

When you have enough clarity that your awareness of your chosen object stops completely fading out periodically, you've reached the fifth milestone. For the first time, you have enough attentional stability and clarity that you get a continuous view of your chosen object (that persists for some duration of your choosing); your view is no longer interrupted by complete distraction or complete dullness. (However, partial distraction and partial dullness persist. Partial distraction was described in the previous chapter; in *partial dullness,* your awareness of your chosen object periodically fades out partially, but not completely.)

Reaching the fifth milestone is a significant accomplishment! In my daily meditation sessions (outside of a retreat context), I consider it a good session when I can reach the fifth milestone. To test whether you've reached it, ask yourself, "Has my experience of this object been *completely* interrupted by distraction or dullness recently?" If so, you're not at the fifth milestone yet.

THE INTERMEDIATE CONCENTRATION MILESTONES

On your way *to* the intermediate milestones, you overcame complete distraction and complete dullness. Now, as you *traverse* the *intermediate concentration milestones,* you'll overcome *partial* distraction and *partial* dullness. The following are the intermediate milestones:

- **5th milestone:** Your chosen object no longer completely fades out; however, you still get partially distracted, and your chosen object still partially fades out.
- **6th milestone:** You no longer get partially distracted; however, you still get subtly distracted, and your chosen object still partially fades out.
- **7th milestone:** Your chosen object no longer partially fades out; however, you still get subtly distracted, and your chosen object still subtly fades out.

CHOOSING AN OBJECT OF ATTENTION

To traverse these milestones, there are at least two ways to go in terms of choosing an object of attention: you can keep working with the breath (or the sign, if it has appeared), or you can take your current field of subjective experience as your chosen object (as described in the section that follows). Each route has its advantages.

The breath (and the sign) are a lot less expansive than your current field of experience, so it can be easier to attend to them as you develop the increased stability and clarity that's required to traverse the intermediate milestones; however, working with the breath (or the sign) won't do much to help you develop attentional expansiveness. For developing expansiveness, your current field of experience is an excellent object to work with. I suggest you do what I've done: experiment with each object at different times, to get some experience working with each of them.

EXPANDING YOUR FIELD OF VIEW

As I describe in chapter 6 (in the section "Four Aspects of Attention"), I find it helpful to distinguish between expansiveness and range of attention. If attention were a beam of light and your experiences were spread across a landscape, your attentional expansiveness would be your ability to widen that beam, and your attentional range would correspond to the portion of the landscape that you know how to light up.

Now that you've developed a basic level of attentional stability and clarity, you can consider adding expansiveness to the mix. Think of your field of experience as a space in which many types of phenomena arise: thoughts, feelings, sensations, and more. Note that *everything* you've ever experienced (and everything you ever *will* experience) arises within that space. This practice involves expanding your field of view to rest your attention on *everything that's currently arising* within that space—taking your *current field of experience* as your object of attention.

Expand your field of view *gently*, without exceeding your capacities for attentional expansiveness or range. (If you push too hard and exceed your capacities, you'll start losing attentional stability. In chapter 10, in the section "Building Expansiveness and Range," I suggest practices for increasing your capacities for expansiveness and range, but here, stability and clarity are priorities.) Attend to what's *already arising* in experience. (Don't try to make additional phenomena arise; phenomena will arise on their own, without any effort required.)

After expanding your field of view, you must prevent it from collapsing. Use introspection as a quality control mechanism to monitor the expansiveness of your attention. Don't allow your attention to collapse onto *any particular phenomenon* that arises. When your attention collapses, this is a form of distraction that interferes with your attentional stability; if you're noting distraction, you might note "distraction" when you notice that your attention has collapsed.

Your attention may collapse onto things you're thinking about, sensations you're experiencing, or anything else. (If you're like me, your attention is most likely to collapse onto things you're thinking about.) Note that for this practice, you *don't* need to stop thinking —you just need to prevent your field of view from collapsing. Having thoughts is okay as long as you can keep your field of view expanded to include other phenomena beyond what you're thinking about (your sensations, for instance). Don't let your thinking run wild, and don't think *intentionally,* but don't put a lot of effort into trying to *stop* thinking, either. If you're able to maintain the expansiveness of your attention, your thinking will settle down on its own, over time.

Once you grow accustomed to this practice, you can try taking your current field of experience as your chosen object at the beginning of a meditation session (as you traverse the beginning milestones). However, there's a risk in doing that: as you traverse the beginning milestones, you have so little attentional stability and clarity that it can be easy to fool yourself into believing you've been *including* thinking in an expanded field of view when your attention has actually *collapsed* onto the things you're thinking about. For this reason, I usually choose a simpler object for traversing the beginning milestones (unless I'm feeling especially confident).

Note that some phenomena arise in the center of your field of view; these tend to be more vivid. Other phenomena arise at the edges of your field of view; these tend to be *less* vivid. To cultivate attentional clarity when doing this practice, do so by raising the level of energy going into your attention across your entire field of view. As you do so, you'll notice that phenomena toward the center of your field of view get a lot more vivid, and phenomena at the edges of your field of view get a little more vivid (but are still somewhat fuzzy). Don't try to make your entire field of view completely vivid; in my experience, there will always be fuzzy phenomena at its edges.

IN OTHER FRAMEWORKS

This practice seems related to the Tibetan Buddhist practice of *settling the mind in its natural state.*

TRAVERSING THE INTERMEDIATE MILESTONES

Traversing the intermediate milestones requires less effort than traversing the beginning milestones. To traverse the intermediate milestones, there are two issues you need to deal with: partial distraction and partial dullness. Tackle partial distraction first. Use introspection (and possibly noting) to help you notice it; when you do, return your attention to your chosen object.

In partial distraction, *most* of your attention is on what's distracting you while *some* of your attention remains on your chosen object. You've reached the sixth milestone when you have enough attentional stability that the reverse becomes true: when you get distracted, *some* of your attention is on what's distracting you while *most* of your attention remains on your chosen object. (This is *subtle distraction*).

At this level of attentional stability, your thinking will have slowed down significantly, you will become aware of your thoughts earlier in their formation than you did when traversing the beginning milestones, and your thoughts will probably seem less distinct

—more like faint, echoing concepts than distinct phrases. You may be tempted to try to notice each thought at the moment that it arises; however, if your experience is like mine, you will discover that this is a futile effort because thoughts don't just suddenly arise —they gradually fade in, with no clear beginning point. The earlier you notice them, the fainter and less distinct they appear.

The next issue to tackle is partial dullness, in which your awareness of your chosen object periodically fades out partially, but not completely. Use introspection (and possibly noting) to help you notice partial dullness; when you notice it, raise the level of energy going into your attention to counteract it.

You've reached the seventh milestone when your perception of your chosen object is almost completely stable and clear, but not quite; the defects that remain are subtle distraction and *subtle dullness* (meaning occasional, barely perceptible fade-outs of your awareness of your chosen object).

Note that complete, partial, and subtle distraction are on a continuum—they aren't discrete phenomena—so don't get too distracted by trying to categorize what type of distraction you're experiencing! The same goes for dullness.

EXPERIENCES YOU MAY HAVE

At low levels of concentration, an incessant flow of involuntary thoughts maintains your familiar sense of self and reality. At an intermediate level of concentration, this flow of involuntary thoughts slows down—so it shouldn't be surprising that when you reach the intermediate milestones, you may start experiencing some unusual phenomena. The following are examples of the diverse phenomena I've experienced around these milestones (and beyond).

Relaxation and Bliss

When I reach the intermediate milestones, there's often a noticeable transition in my state. Suddenly, my body seems to start spontaneously letting go of areas of muscular tension, I start noticing my heartbeat, I feel somewhat blissful, and a smile may appear on my face. This transition is a pleasant experience, and in general, meditation is much more pleasant around the intermediate milestones than around the beginning milestones.

At this level of concentration, meditation can be quite a restful, healing experience. Don't be ashamed to sink in and soak up the pleasant feelings! Doing so can be a great support for your vitality. Try taking your current experiences of bodily bliss as your object of attention, and notice what happens over time. (I can often find subtle experiences of bliss around my hands and arms at this level of concentration.)

Tension Releases and Energy Surges

In addition to the more generalized relaxation and bliss that I describe above, in most meditation sessions in which I reach an intermediate level of concentration, I start noticing a more specific process of tension release. When I'm taking my current field of experience as my chosen object, the following pattern often shows up repeatedly within each session:

1. I notice an area of tension that had previously been outside my field of view.
2. I expand my field of view to include that tension.
3. Within a short time—often, within seconds—the tension spontaneously releases and I feel energized.

The tension could be somatic, emotional, and/or intellectual. I often have some resistance to including the tension in my field of view; I don't really want to look at it, and the idea of looking at it brings up anxiety. This anxiety is uncomfortable, and when I do look at the tension, experiencing it can also be uncomfortable.

When the tension spontaneously releases, I experience this release as an increase in vitality that can manifest somatically (as relaxation and bliss), emotionally (as relief and happiness), and/or intellectually (as increased understanding). The release in tension is often accompanied by a pleasant energy surge in which my arms want to shake and my toes want to wiggle; when I'm meditating alone, I let them do so (rather than trying to hold still).

Awareness can be a powerful healing force; at intermediate levels of concentration, as your awareness starts to get free from the demands of involuntary thinking, it can start spontaneously serving your healing and growth. I believe this is the process at work in most contemporary mindfulness-based psychological approaches to stress reduction and healing.

(The meditative experience of release of tension seems related to psychologist Peter Levine's concept of *pendulation*.)

MEMORIES

For a few months after I first reached the intermediate milestones, when I reached these milestones in my meditation sessions, I'd often start noticing a stream of memories showing up in my mind's eye in the form of rapidly evolving images. Ken Wilber has described meditation experiences like this as "being at the movies." It's as if my mind had a backlog of unprocessed material; as soon as I gave my mind a break from all the thinking I'd been doing, my mind seized this opportunity to get to work on processing that backlog.

I found this process interesting, engaging, and pleasant. Memories arose that I hadn't thought of for decades. Rather than trying to stop these memories from arising, I expanded my field of view to include them (as described earlier in this chapter in the section "Choosing an Object of Attention") and I let them play themselves out. Eventually, they stopped arising.

FACES

As the rational functions of my intellect start going off-line at intermediate levels of concentration, I sometimes notice more primitive, dreamlike phenomena arising. This can lead to some fairly unusual experiences.

One of the first such experiences that I noticed was an experience of faces showing up in patterns on the floor. One moment, I'd be looking at a random pattern in the carpet or on the floorboards; the next moment, the pattern would resolve into primitive, cartoon-like representations of human and animal faces exhibiting a wide range of expressions.

These faces would be quite striking, often disturbing, and very difficult to ignore. Trying to make them go away didn't help. What *did* help was to simply let them be as they were and to continue my meditation practice; the faces always went away by the end of the session. After a number of years, this phenomenon subsided—perhaps not coincidentally, it subsided around the time that I resolved some challenging emotional material I'd been working with.

DREAMS

Sometimes, as I'm meditating, I notice that I've slipped into an actual dream state (without actually falling asleep). Usually, as soon as I notice this (and become lucid), the dream state ends and I return to my previous meditative state. I've sometimes explored whether I can sustain this state of lucid dreaming within a meditation session, but I haven't had any success with this as of this writing.

EMOTIONALLY-CHARGED IMAGES

Occasionally, I've noticed emotionally-charged images arising as I meditate. These images have generally arisen spontaneously and unintentionally. Some of these images have felt like benevolent guardians; my experiences of these images have been intensely meaningful and heart-opening. Other images have had an electric, demonic quality that I've experienced as simultaneously scary and seductive.

Rather than turning away from these images, I've made it a practice to turn *toward* them instead, allowing myself to fully *experience* them (while taking care not to identify with them or allow my attention to collapse onto them). When I've done this, inevitably, these images have soon dissolved into energy—often, *a lot* of energy. This has often been a healing, integrative experience for me; I believe it's an intense version of the tension release process that I described earlier in this section.

❧❦

If you've had unusual experiences related to meditation, you're not alone; in her research project, The Difficult Stages of the Contemplative Path, neuroscience researcher Willoughby Britton has cataloged many unusual experiences people have had while meditating in various contexts. If you notice unpleasant experiences arising that seem related to your meditation practice, and if you're concerned about these experiences, it may be a good idea to slow down or pause your meditation practice and seek advice from someone you trust. (If the only advice you ever receive from them is "just keep meditating," I suggest you seek advice from someone else!)

Meditative experiences can be compelling and captivating, and certain meditative experiences, like the sign, can serve as indicators of your current degree of concentration. Because of these factors, it's easy to become overly concerned with what meditative experiences you're having (or not having) while you're in the midst of concentration meditation. When I notice that this is happening to me, I find it helpful to remind myself that fundamentally, concentration is about *how you attend*—not *what you experience*. No sign? No bliss? Having a bad day? Don't worry about it… if concentration practice is what you've chosen to do, just *do the practice*, and don't try to force any particular experience to happen.

Use introspection to notice how you're attending. What's your attention *doing?* Are you able to rest your attention on your chosen object, or are you distracted? Are you experiencing your chosen object vividly and continuously, or is your experience dull and interrupted? In concentration meditation, these issues are much more important than whether or not you're experiencing any particular phenomena.

SUMMARY

To get from the last beginning milestone to the first intermediate milestone, you must raise your level of attentional clarity. When you have enough clarity that your awareness of your chosen object stops completely fading out periodically, you've reached the intermediate milestones; for the first time, you have enough attentional stability and clarity that you get a continuous view of your chosen object (that persists for some duration of your choosing); your view is no longer interrupted by complete distraction or complete dullness.

As you traverse the *intermediate concentration milestones,* you overcome partial distraction and *partial dullness* (in which your awareness of your chosen object periodically fades out partially, but not completely). You can keep working with the breath (or the sign, if it has appeared) as your object of attention, or you can take your current field of subjective experience as your chosen object.

At the last of the intermediate milestones, your perception of your chosen object is almost completely stable and clear, but not quite; the defects that remain are *subtle distraction* (when some of your attention is on what's distracting you while most of your attention remains on your chosen object) and *subtle dullness* (meaning occasional, barely perceptible fade-outs of your awareness of your chosen object).

As you traverse the intermediate milestones, you may experience some unusual phenomena, including relaxation and bliss, tension releases, energy surges, memories, faces, dreams, and emotionally-charged images. If you have unpleasant experiences that seem related to your meditation practice, slow down or pause your meditation practice and seek advice from someone you trust.

CHAPTER 9

MASTER SINGLE-POINTED ATTENTION

TO GET FROM the seventh milestone (the last intermediate milestone) to the eighth milestone (the first advanced milestone), you must raise your level of attentional stability and clarity enough to resolve the final attentional issues that remain: subtle distraction and subtle dullness. Only minimal effort is required to do this; as you notice subtle distraction, involuntary thinking will spontaneously dissipate, and as you notice subtle dullness, your attention will spontaneously clarify. You don't have to stop thoughts from arising, but you do have to stop getting *distracted by* your thoughts—that is, your attention needs to stop getting diverted by (and collapsing onto) the things you're thinking about.

When you've resolved subtle distraction and subtle dullness, you've reached the eighth milestone, and you experience *single-pointed attention*—that is, attention that's completely stable and clear. (The term *single-pointed* doesn't refer to the expansiveness of your attention; for instance, if you take your entire field of experience as your object of attention, the single "point" that you attend to here is quite expansive.) To test whether you've reached the eighth milestone, the relevant question to ask yourself is, "Has my attention been completely stable and clear (for a time duration of your choosing)?" Equivalently, you can ask, "Have I experienced any distraction or dullness whatsoever (over that time duration)?" Use introspection to find out. (The time duration is an important consideration, as described in the section "Measuring Concentration" in chapter 7. It can be fairly easy to achieve complete stability and clarity at will *for a short duration;* however, *sustaining* that stability and clarity over a longer duration is much more challenging and results in much deeper levels of concentration.)

As with the transition from the beginning to the intermediate milestones, I sometimes experience a noticeable change in state as I transition from the intermediate to the advanced milestones. This feels like a marble rolling into an indentation on the surface of a table; first, I sense the indentation, then I intentionally move toward it and—within a second or two—land in it. At that point, I sense a noticeable increase in the stability of both my attention and my state of mind.

As of this writing, on a good day, I find I'm sometimes able to reach the advanced milestones (using a brief time duration criteria of a few minutes) within an hour of meditation in my daily practice routine (outside of a retreat context)—*provided that* I'm also doing some mindfulness practice interspersed in daily life. If I neglect mindfulness in my daily life, I generally don't have enough momentum to reach the advanced milestones in my formal practice sessions.

THE ADVANCED CONCENTRATION MILESTONES

As you traverse the *advanced concentration milestones,* (moving from the eighth to the ninth milestone), you learn to effortlessly maintain single-pointed attention. The following are the advanced milestones:

- **8ᵗʰ milestone:** Your attention is *single-pointed* (completely stable and clear); however, it requires some effort to maintain this state.
- **9ᵗʰ milestone:** You can effortlessly maintain single-pointed attention.

At the eighth milestone, your *attention* is already completely stable —meaning that you don't get distracted—however, the effort that's required to *sustain* this state of single-pointed attention makes the *state itself* somewhat unstable. Releasing this effort increases the stability of the state. When you use introspection to look for defects in your state of concentration, you will recognize effort as an unpleasant defect. Just as with distraction and dullness, as you notice your effort, it dissipates.

BEYOND THE ADVANCED MILESTONES

If you reach the ninth milestone and you're interested in taking your concentration practice further, there are at least two ways you could go: you could learn to rest at the ninth milestone for longer periods of time, or you could seek further concentration goals *beyond* the ninth milestone. (Two resources that describe such goals are B. Alan Wallace's book *The Attention Revolution* and section 1 of Shaila Catherine's book *Wisdom Wide and Deep*.) Personally, I've found the nine milestones defined in this book to be sufficient for the range of concentration states that I tend to encounter in my daily practice routine.

SUMMARY

To get from the last intermediate milestone to the first advanced milestone, you must raise your level of attentional stability and clarity enough to resolve subtle distraction and subtle dullness. As

you notice subtle distraction, involuntary thinking will spontaneously dissipate, and as you notice subtle dullness, your attention
will spontaneously clarify. At this point, you've reached the first of
the advanced milestones, and you experience *single-pointed attention*—that is, attention that's completely stable and clear.

As you traverse the *advanced concentration milestones*, you learn
to effortlessly maintain single-pointed attention; you release the effort that's required to sustain this state, which increases the stability
of the state.

CHAPTER 10

LEARN ADDITIONAL MINDFULNESS PRACTICES

D AILY CONCENTRATION meditation sessions will help you build a firm foundation of mindfulness; however, beyond concentration practice, there's more you can (and should) do to cultivate mindfulness.

DOING-NOTHING MEDITATION

Sometimes, you'll find that your level of concentration is so low that you're barely able to remember your object of attention at all, and you're unable to make any progress through the concentration milestones. At times like these, instead of doing concentration practice, I find it helpful to do a very different meditation practice that I call *doing-nothing meditation*. The instructions for this practice are quite simple: when you notice yourself trying to do *anything*—including trying to stop thinking—let go of the doing.

Don't be fooled by the simplicity of these instructions; this is a powerful mindfulness practice that's worth exploring in addition to —or even *instead of*—concentration practice. However, I suggest you gain some experience with concentration practice before you try this practice.

BUILDING EXPANSIVENESS AND RANGE

So far, we've mostly been focusing on attentional stability and clarity; however, two other important aspects of mindfulness that you shouldn't neglect are expansiveness and range. In concentration practice, you *can* cultivate expansiveness (as described in chapter 8 in the section "Expanding Your Field of View"); however, attentional stability and clarity are the priorities there. Outside of concentration practice, you can do mindfulness practices designed specifically for cultivating expansiveness and range *(expansiveness practices* and *range practices);* you can do these either as formal meditations or informally, in the midst of daily life.

EXPANSIVENESS PRACTICES

To increase your capacity for attentional expansiveness:

1. Choose a nonconceptual focal point to start from and direct your attention there.
2. Gradually and methodically expand your attentional field of view to encompass more of your current field of experience —while maintaining attentional clarity—until you feel a comfortable stretch.
3. Rest your attention there.

For instance, let's say you start by directing your attention to the center of your visual field. From there, you might gradually expand your attentional field of view to encompass more of your visual field. Eventually, you're clearly aware of your entire visual field; at this point, if this seems like enough of a stretch for now, you might choose to rest your attention there for a while. On the other hand, you could also choose to continue to expand your attentional field to include other sensory modalities or other types of experiences. For instance, a combination I like to work with is everything I see, everything I hear, and everything I feel in my body. (The expansiveness practices in this section have been informed by the published work of Buddhist teacher Ken McLeod.)

RANGE PRACTICES

What makes exploring reality exciting? Its limitless nature: the more you look, the more you find. Doing range practices is another form of exploring: it's exploring *your field of subjective experience.* If you're like me, your field of subjective experience may not seem that interesting to explore at first glance because *you think you already know what's there:* for instance, you may think that what you'll find there are your five senses and your thoughts. However, the more I've explored subjective experience, the more I've become convinced that subjective experience is just as limitless as reality.

Increasing your attentional range isn't a matter of trying to *make new experiences arise* (though you will certainly *have* new experiences as you expand your attentional range); doing range practices is more about *discovering* (and making sense of) unfamiliar *types of experience* that are *already arising* in your field of subjective experience. For instance, you don't need to take up scuba diving to increase your attentional range; you can do range practices right on your familiar meditation seat.

A great time to do range practices is right after you've done some concentration practice; at that time, you'll be able to focus on unfamiliar regions of experience with more clarity and less distraction. To increase your attentional range:

1. Seek out a region of your current field of experience that seems vague, fuzzy, or in shadow.
2. Shine the light of your attention on this region to discover what's there.
3. Rest your attention there and watch what unfolds.
4. Afterward, make sense of what you've experienced.

The last step—making sense of what you've experienced—is an important part of the practice; integrating unfamiliar types of experience into your worldview is essential for making them more familiar (and thus more easily accessed). Rather than reinventing the wheel, it can be helpful to do some research to discover how *others* have made sense of the types of experience you're exploring. Your research can serve as a guide for deepening your exploration and discovering additional unfamiliar areas to explore.

To get you started, here are some examples of types of experience that I've explored as I've increased my attentional range:

- Smells
- Body sensations
- Feelings and emotions
- Impulses
- Nonconceptual experiences associated with relationships
- Dream-like, sub-rational phenomena
- Subtle feelings of energy in and around the body
- Synchronicities

CULTIVATING MINDFULNESS IN DAILY LIFE

Formal meditation practice is essential for cultivating mindfulness; however, with formal practice as a foundation, you can enhance your practice routine by integrating informal mindfulness practices into your daily life. Informal practice is especially helpful if you do most of your spiritual practices outside of a retreat context (as I do); informal practice can help you avoid losing mindfulness between formal practice sessions.

Without informal mindfulness practice, I find that I spend an inordinate amount of time and energy engaged in involuntary, unproductive thinking in my daily life. Informal mindfulness practice helps me reduce this unproductive thinking. Not only does this have a positive impact on my productivity, it also frees my attention so I can have a much richer, deeper experience of life—thus supporting my vitality, too.

INTROSPECTION AND NOTING

One easy way to integrate mindfulness practice into your daily life is by periodically doing some introspection and noting as you carry out the activities of daily life. For instance, you could investigate what your attention and intellect are up to, clarify what you actually *want* to be attending to, and note distraction and dullness. To make this a habit, try setting a timer to periodically remind yourself to do this. (Introspection and noting are described in chapter 7, in the section "Using Introspection and Noting.")

MINDFULNESS CHAINING

For many daily activities (like brushing your teeth or doing the dishes), little or no thinking is required—and if you're like me, you may find that the thinking you *do* end up doing during these activities isn't very helpful. Doing these activities can be a great time for informal mindfulness practice.

One way I help increase my level of mindfulness during these activities is through an informal practice that I call *mindfulness chaining:* I'll ask myself what I need to do next, I'll choose a small task that will take a minute or less to complete, and I'll set an intention to stay mindful (that is, to maintain a stable, clear, expansive awareness of a wide range of my current experiences) *as* I do that task. As soon as that task is complete, I immediately repeat this process, asking myself what I need to do next and setting an intention to stay mindful as I do it. (The recurring, rhythmic aspect of this practice helps you remember to do the practice; in this sense, it's like counting breaths in formal concentration practice.)

A side benefit of mindfulness chaining is that my productivity increases; I find that I do my tasks much more energetically and efficiently since my energy isn't being drained by involuntary thinking.

EXPANDING ATTENTION BEYOND YOUR THOUGHTS

You can also do the above practices at times when your intellect *is* engaged—during activities like reading, writing, talking with others, and making decisions; however, this can be a lot more challenging.

Often, when we think, our attention collapses onto the things we're thinking about. To help maintain the expansiveness of your attention, you can practice thinking while simultaneously using introspection to notice (and maintain some awareness of) your current subjective *experience* of thinking. It can also help to expand your field of view to include other sensations. You can even try taking your entire field of experience as an object of attention as you do activities that require intellectual engagement.

SUMMARY

Beyond concentration practice, there's more you can (and should) do to cultivate mindfulness.

Sometimes, your level of concentration is so low that you're unable to make progress through the concentration milestones. At times like these, instead of doing concentration practice, try *doing-nothing meditation:* when you notice yourself trying to do anything —including trying to stop thinking—let go of the doing.

Concentration builds attentional stability and clarity; you can also do practices specifically for cultivating attentional expansiveness and range *(expansiveness practices* and *range practices)*.

With formal practice as a foundation, you can enhance your practice routine by integrating informal mindfulness practices into your daily life; these practices can help you reduce unproductive thinking, raising your productivity and freeing your attention so you can have a richer, deeper experience of life. An easy way to do this is by periodically doing some introspection and noting as you carry out the activities of daily life. You can also do *mindfulness chaining:* setting an intention to stay mindful (that is, to maintain a stable, clear, expansive awareness of a wide range of your current experiences) as you do successive tasks.

You can do informal mindfulness practices at times when your intellect is engaged—during activities like reading, writing, talking with others, and making decisions. To help maintain the expansiveness of your attention, practice thinking while simultaneously using introspection to notice (and maintain some awareness of) your current subjective experience of thinking. It can also help to expand your field of view to include other sensations.

❧❦

So far, you've developed a spiritual practice routine and learned how to use concentration and other meditation practices to cultivate mindfulness. Part 3 builds on this foundation, showing how you can use additional meditation practices to transcend self and reality by cultivating insight (an experiential understanding of the relationships between self, reality, awareness, and subjective experience).

PART THREE

CULTIVATE INSIGHT

CHAPTER 11

UNDERSTAND INSIGHT

O UR CONCEPTUAL FACULTIES give us the power to think, to reason, and to make sense of life. As we grow, our developing conceptual faculties give us increasingly sophisticated abilities to understand and perceive ourselves and reality. However, we pay a price for this power: we become increasingly identified with conceptual constructs, and our experience of life becomes increasingly filtered through conceptual understanding. We unconsciously make up a story that explains life (that is, our experiences), then we lose track of *life* and focus all our attention on the *story*. Insight reminds us that the story is just a story.

Insight practice involves examining (and revising) stories that affect our perception of several fundamental aspects of life. More precisely, *insight practice* is the experiential exploration of the relationships between self, reality, awareness, and subjective experience. The result of insight practice is *insight,* which is both an understanding of those relationships and an ability to access modes of perception in which those relationships are evident.

(Besides being informed by personal experience, my views on cultivating insight have also been informed by the published work of Buddhist teacher Ken McLeod, my experiences with meditation instructor Kenneth Folk, and my experiences with the Karma Kagyu lineage of Tibetan Buddhism. However, the views expressed in this book are my own; they are not intended to represent the views of any other persons, traditions, religions, lineages, organizations, or professions that I may be associated with.)

IN OTHER FRAMEWORKS

The concept of *insight,* as I've defined it, seems closely related to the concept of *vipassana* or *vipasyana*—often translated as *insight*—in Buddhism.

INSIGHT AND COGNITION

I've heard it said that insight can't be understood. It might be more accurate to say that understanding insight isn't sufficient for attaining it. That's because insight isn't just a shift in understanding; it's also a shift in perception. Perception is a deeply ingrained habit, and cultivating a shift in perception requires *practice* (not just conceptual learning and understanding). This makes insight distinct from philosophy.

Personally, I've found that having an understanding of insight *has* helped me cultivate it; if you want to get somewhere, it helps to understand where you're going. I've also found descriptions of insight helpful as a *measure* of insight; as I've gained deeper levels of insight, descriptions of insight that had previously seemed paradoxical have started to make sense. However, be aware that you can *study* insight forever and never actually *achieve* insight—so if you want to achieve it, spend time on spiritual *practice* (not just spiritual study).

Insight is primarily *cognitive,* in that it impacts our understanding and perception of the *relationships* between phenomena; insight itself doesn't fundamentally alter our nonconceptual experiences. For instance, when you look at a tree, the nonconceptual aspects of your visual experience are going to be more or less the same with and without insight. (The tree isn't going to be a different color with insight.) However, the understandings and perceptions that arise *related to* your visual experience of the tree may be quite different with insight.

That being said, insight *can* affect nonconceptual experience in at least a couple of ways. Intermediate and advanced levels of insight direct our attention to subjective experience; this can help us perceive experience more clearly and vividly. Intermediate and advanced levels of insight can also break down conceptual barriers that limit our perception of phenomena (both conceptual and nonconceptual); this can free us to perceive phenomena we couldn't perceive before. In these ways, insight can support mindfulness by increasing the clarity and range of our awareness.

BENEFITS OF INSIGHT

For me, insight practice has led to a dramatic and welcome reduction in my overall level of anxiety. It's not that I have no fear—I'm still afraid of plenty—but insight has reduced my fear of being worthless and my fear of not existing. Insight practice reveals a number of unconventional ways of understanding and perceiving ourselves—ways in which we become less subject to negative self-evaluation and fear of non-existence. This frees us to respond less reactively to life's challenges. If a mountain lion were chasing me through the forest, would I feel afraid of being eaten? You bet! Would I feel afraid of ceasing to exist after death? Less so now than before I started doing insight practice.

For those of us who value truth, insight practice offers another benefit: intermediate and advanced levels of insight practice can help you discover *the truth about truth*—transcending and including *conceptual understanding itself.* (You *transcend* it in that you free yourself and your experience of life from unconscious embeddedness in conceptual constructs, and you *include* it in that after insight, all the power of conceptual understanding remains available to you.) With insight, you don't *lose* your conceptual faculties—you shift your *relationship* to them; conceptual understanding becomes your *servant* (rather than your master). (Thanks to Ken Wilber for the *transcend and include* model of development.)

Risks of Insight Practice

This section describes important cautions that you should be aware of before starting insight practice. Cultivating insight can be disturbing. At advanced levels, insight practice invites us to step out of the familiar conceptual matrix that we developed in; when we accept that invitation, we enter a conceptual free fall in which nothing is certain.

Insight practices have the potential to be psychologically destabilizing. The aim of insight practice is *not* to weaken your ability to cope with life or to make you lose touch with reality. If any of that seems to be happening, use your judgment about how to proceed, and consider seeking guidance from a mental health professional or someone else whose advice you trust; it may be that at this time, your awakening would be best served by cultivating other aspects of awakening (such as vitality, mindfulness, and compassion) rather than insight—or, it may be that you simply need to take a break and regain your balance before proceeding.

For some, insight practice causes problems; for others, it doesn't. The more mindfulness and psychological health that you bring to insight practice, the safer and more effective your insight practices will be. In my own insight practices, I've experienced awe, joy, and exhilaration; I've also had experiences that have been less pleasant: temporary states of fear, nausea, confusion, disorientation, and dissociation. In addition, I've had a number of intense dreams that seem related to my insight practices.

SEVEN LEVELS OF INSIGHT

I believe insight is best cultivated in a series of levels over which understanding and perception become successively more refined. The following are the *levels of insight* I've identified. (I've named each level for the phenomenon that's the central focus of that level and, after the name, I've briefly described the experience that's characteristic of each level.)

1. Reality. (You're real.)
2. Interdependence. (You're one with reality.)
3. Witnessing. (You're the witness.)
4. Presence. (Reality arises in present experience.)
5. Evenness. (Awareness and experience are one.)
6. Experience only. (Experience is.)
7. No reference. (There's no ultimate frame of reference.)

(I don't claim that these levels are the only ones possible or that they can only be accessed in this sequence. However, in my experience of cultivating insight, I *did* access these levels in roughly this order, and I believe this sequence of levels can serve as a helpful framework for cultivating insight.)

Each level of insight has:

- a corresponding **conceptual framework** (or *view*),
- a corresponding **state of mind**, and
- a corresponding set of **experiences** (that differentiate that state of mind from others).

For some levels, I've also identified a corresponding set of **spiritual practices.** In the following chapters, I describe the view, practices, state of mind, and experiences associated with each level of insight.

Cultivating each level of insight requires study, practice, and assessment:

- **Study** is required to familiarize yourself with the view, practices, and experiences associated with the level of insight you're cultivating.
- **Practice** is required to develop the ability to use the view and any associated practices to shift your perception and enter the associated state of mind.
- **Assessment** is required to make sense of your practice experiences, to determine the extent to which you've entered the state of mind you've been intending to enter, and to create plans for further study and practice.

Since perception is a deeply ingrained habit, shifting how you perceive can take a significant amount of practice. So, even after the *view* of a given level of insight makes perfect sense to you, you'll probably still need a lot of practice to enter the *state* corresponding to that level. Study, alone, generally isn't enough.

SUMMARY

Insight practice involves examining (and revising) stories that affect our perception of several fundamental aspects of life. More precisely, *insight practice* is the experiential exploration of the relationships between self, reality, awareness, and subjective experience. The result of insight practice is *insight*, which is both an understanding of those relationships and an ability to access modes of perception in which those relationships are evident.

Understanding insight isn't sufficient for attaining it. That's because insight isn't just a shift in understanding; it's also a shift in perception. Cultivating a shift in perception requires practice (not just conceptual learning and understanding). This makes insight distinct from philosophy.

Insight is primarily cognitive, in that it impacts our understanding and perception of the relationships between phenomena; insight itself doesn't fundamentally alter our nonconceptual experiences.

Insight practice has a number of benefits: it can support mindfulness by increasing the clarity and range of your awareness, it can reduce anxiety, and it can help you discover *the truth about truth*. With insight, you don't lose your conceptual faculties—you shift your relationship to them; conceptual understanding becomes your servant (rather than your master).

Cultivating insight can be disturbing, and insight practices have the potential to be psychologically destabilizing. The aim of insight practice is *not* to weaken your ability to cope with life or to make you lose touch with reality; if any of that seems to be happening, consider seeking guidance from a mental health professional or someone else whose advice you trust. The more mindfulness and psychological health that you bring to insight practice, the safer and more effective your insight practices will be.

I believe insight is best cultivated in a series of levels over which understanding and perception become successively more refined. The following are the levels of insight I've identified: reality, interdependence, witnessing, presence, evenness, experience only, and no reference. Each level of insight has a corresponding conceptual framework (or *view)*, a corresponding state of mind, and a corresponding set of experiences. For some levels, I've also identified a corresponding set of spiritual practices.

Cultivating each level of insight requires study, practice, and assessment. Since perception is a deeply ingrained habit, shifting how you perceive can take a significant amount of practice; even after the *view* of a given level of insight makes perfect sense to you, you'll probably still need a lot of practice to enter the *state* corresponding to that level.

CHAPTER 12

TRANSCEND REALITY

I N THIS CHAPTER and the next, we explore the view, state of mind, and experiences associated with each of the seven levels of insight that I've identified. At the beginning of this exploration, we believe we're *part of* reality. After articulating what *reality* means and exploring various ways of grounding yourself *in* reality (in levels 1 and 2), this chapter shows how to shift your sense of self *beyond* reality (in level 3). From this vantage point, it becomes possible to view subjective experience as *more fundamental* than reality (in level 4); this inversion in how we normally understand experience and reality prepares the way for transcending self (as described in the next chapter).

LEVEL 1: REALITY

As I define it, *reality* is the set of phenomena perceived both by you and by others who share your worldview. Your *worldview* is a set of interrelated concepts (a frame of reference) that supports your perception of reality. (I discuss frames of reference in more detail in the section "Level 7: No Reference" below). Different worldviews may support the perception of vastly different phenomena: matter, space, time, energy, life, consciousness, human needs, unconscious psychological forces, souls, God, gods and demons, heaven and hell, and more—there's room for *all* phenomena across the diversity of our worldviews.

At level 1—the *reality level*—you perceive yourself to be a part of reality (whatever reality consists of for you). Maybe you're a physical body on a journey from birth to death. Maybe you're a soul on a journey from young to old, inhabiting many bodies along the way. There are many possible worldviews; you hold one of these views and you pay attention to what's real (in your view).

Your view of what's real informs your values and governs your understanding of yourself (your *real self*, that is—more on that in the next section!) Your view of what's real allows you to discover important truths about life and allows you to communicate and collaborate with others who share a similar view. However, your view of reality also *hides* important truths—truths that don't fit within your view of what's real. At this level, if you understand yourself to be a temporary phenomenon in an ever-changing reality, you may experience a fear of eventual nonexistence.

This level may not seem very significant in terms of insight; however, reaching this level is quite an accomplishment in terms of mental health and the ability to function in life. In the framework of mental health, experiencing reality as unreal is known as *derealization,* experiencing oneself as unreal is known as *depersonalization,* and not being able to distinguish what's real from what's not is known as *psychosis* (not to be confused with *psychopathy); *these can be scary, disturbing, and debilitating experiences. If you suffer from any of these experiences, get support from a mental health professional—hopefully, one whose worldview is similar to yours—and don't proceed with insight practice until you are solidly grounded in reality.

The reality level encompasses a vast array of frames of reference; what they all have in common is a focus on reality (as opposed to subjective experience) as their organizing principle. All phenomena are reduced to—or described in terms of—reality (not subjective experience); subjective experience is ignored, minimized, or included as part of reality—with reality being the organizing principle and the central focus.

In Other Frameworks

Any spiritual or secular framework that either positions you as *part of* reality or ignores your *relationship to* reality is operating at this first level of insight. Such frameworks are commonly found in science, materialism, atheism, theism, non-mystical forms of religion, and non-mystical new age spirituality. Examples of such frameworks include scientific frameworks that describe consciousness as an *epiphenomenon of* reality and science-flavored spiritual frameworks that include consciousness as a *force within* reality. (In science, the concept *nature* is generally synonymous with *reality.)*

Spiritual practices (including "insight" practices) that investigate reality (without exploring the relationship between reality, awareness, and subjective experience) are operating at this first level. Reality is complex, while insight is (relatively) simple. If you're trying to cultivate insight and, in doing so, you find yourself investigating something that seems to be getting more and more complex, you're probably exploring reality—not cultivating insight (as *I* define *insight)*. There's nothing wrong with exploring reality—just be clear about what you're doing.

Level 2: Interdependence

I refer to level 2 as the *interdependence level*. At this level, you perceive yourself *as* reality—*all of* reality. (You perceive others as all of reality, too—so, at this level, you perceive all beings as *one.)* This is actually a special case (or perhaps an advanced sublevel) of the reality level. As such, if you want to, I believe you could skip this level in your process of cultivating insight; however, I do believe cultivating this level can be beneficial.

Remember the self you perceived at the reality level (the self that was a part of reality)? Let's call that self—somewhat ironically—your *real self*. (The *real* in *real self* means "associated with reality"—not "genuine.") Let's call the self you perceive at the interdependence level your *interdependent self*. What happens to your real self once you can perceive yourself as one with reality? Does it still make sense to say and think things like "I'm going to eat dinner now"? Sure; it's just that in this case, "I" refers to your real self (which is a subset of your interdependent self).

To perceive yourself as one with reality, notice the *edges* of your real self, notice the *arbitrariness* of your choice of those edges, and consider more expansive ways of viewing yourself. For instance, do you think you end at your skin? Is the food you eat a part of you after you eat it, and if so, what would it be like to consider it to be a part of you as it's growing in the field? Are your family and friends a part of you? How about your enemies? Would you be the same without them? Could your body and mind exist at all without the rest of reality?

This level can be confused with level 5 (described in the following chapter in the section "Level 5: Evenness"). What this level has in common with level 5 is a focus on union and unity—but this level focuses on reality (rather than awareness and subjective experience) as its organizing principle.

IN OTHER FRAMEWORKS

The term *nondual* has been used to connote various forms of union and unity in various spiritual frameworks; however, because of its ambiguity, I've avoided using the term *nondual* in this model, choosing more specific and descriptive terminology instead.

Mystical forms of religion and spirituality that emphasize interdependence without exploring the relationship between reality and subjectivity are operating at this level of insight.

Concepts related to this level include *pantheism* and *ecosystems*.

LEVEL 3: WITNESSING

Notice that no matter how much your understanding of reality (and your role in it) has changed over time, one thing has always remained the same: you're *aware*. Furthermore, notice that at one level, you perceive yourself to be real—but at a deeper level, you perceive yourself to be *that which is aware*. Recognizing this allows you to access a new way of perceiving yourself; at this third level of insight, you perceive yourself as *the witness* of phenomena—that which is aware. (I refer to this as the *witnessing level*.)

You recognize that although diverse phenomena arise and subside—thoughts, feelings, perceptions, worldviews, and more—awareness itself (as the witness of phenomena) is unchanged and unaffected. This recognition gives you the courage to face difficult experiences since you perceive that these experiences won't fundamentally harm you. Your view of yourself as the witness helps you cultivate deep self-acceptance. The witness is always nonjudgmental because judgment is just another phenomenon arising in awareness. You experience joy in simply being aware.

What happens to the real self at this level? It doesn't disappear; it just becomes another set of phenomena to be witnessed. (The same is true of the interdependent self.) The body, feelings, thoughts, impulses, choices, and actions of the real self arise and subside in awareness, just like all other phenomena. The witness (as I define it) doesn't *make* the choices of the real self; it *witnesses* all the phenomena related to those choices (including thoughts and feelings associated with choice-making).

IN OTHER FRAMEWORKS

This level of insight can be fostered by any psychological or spiritual framework that advocates witnessing as a practice for emotional self-regulation and healing.

LEVEL 4: PRESENCE

We're used to thinking of subjective experience as an insignificant intermediary that lies between what's *really* important: ourselves ("in here") and reality ("out there"). At the fourth level of insight—which I call the *presence level*—our relationship to reality shifts and present-moment subjective experience assumes a much more prominent role.

CONCEPT-FOCUSED VS. EXPERIENCE-FOCUSED PERCEPTION

A mode of perception that should be familiar is *concept-focused* perception, in which:

- Your attention is mainly on conceptual experiences; you may not be aware of your nonconceptual experiences. (I define *conceptual* and *nonconceptual experiences* in the section "Two Flavors of Subjective Experience" in chapter 5.)
- You may not recognize your subjective experience *as* subjective experience.

Cultivating the presence level (and all the levels that follow) requires building the capacity to shift from concept-focused perception to *experience-focused* perception, in which:

- Your attention encompasses both your nonconceptual and conceptual experiences.
- You recognize your subjective experience *as* subjective experience.

(An alternative term for experience-focused perception is *mindfulness of subjective experience*.)

To illustrate this distinction, let's say I happen to glance at a tree in my yard. In concept-focused perception, if I experience anything at all in relation to the tree, it's likely to be thoughts *about it* (such as, "I should really cut that low branch off soon.") On the other hand, in experience-focused perception, I would be aware of both my nonconceptual experiences of the tree (such as my visual experience of it) and my associated conceptual experiences (the knowledge that I'm looking at a tree and the thought "I should really cut that low branch off soon"). Furthermore, I would recognize all of these experiences *as* experiences.

To enter a state of experience-focused perception, try this simple exercise:

1. Walk around. Notice your perception that your body is moving through space as the world around you apparently remains stationary. This is the familiar (concept-focused) mode of perception that corresponds to the reality level.

2. Now, as you continue to walk around, see if you can perceive things another way: notice experiences arising (within your field of experience) as your *field of experience* apparently remains stationary. (This is a more experience-focused mode of perception.) Notice all the types of experience you are having: visual experiences, kinesthetic experiences, auditory experiences, thoughts, emotions, and more. See if you can recognize them all as experiences arising within a "stationary" field of experience (like "moving" images appearing on a stationary movie screen). Recognize all your experiences *as* experiences, as they arise.

3. Practice alternating between these two modes of perception until you can easily switch between them.

4. Now, drop your assumptions about what is "stationary" and see if you can simultaneously perceive your body moving through space and the related experiences arising within your field of experience. Notice that all the familiar perceptions of the reality level arise within *your field of experience*—the broader context that you become aware of at the presence level.

In experience-focused perception, you retain the ability to distinguish your real self from the rest of reality; however, you also gain an ability to view experiences of "in here" and "out there" with a newfound equivalence: you recognize these experiences (and all others) as phenomena arising in your field of experience. Your body, your emotions, and your thoughts all show up as experiences arising—just like your home, your friends, your memories, your plans, and your fantasies. In this sense, experiences of "in here" and "out there" get flattened; they all get flavored by the "one taste" of subjective experience.

REALITY AS AN INTERPRETATION OF EXPERIENCE

The key understanding to cultivate at this level is that you never actually perceive reality directly; all you ever experience is subjective experience. For instance, looking at a chair, you experience a visual experience of the chair—not the chair itself. Touching the chair, you experience a tactile experience of the chair—not the chair itself. You recognize that you've never had—and never *will* have—a direct experience of the "real chair."

You recognize that the existence of the chair in reality isn't a foregone conclusion, but an *interpretation* of your experience based on your worldview—and that other interpretations of your experience are possible. Experience-focused perception helps you recognize that you *construct* your experience of reality as an *interpretation* of your subjective experience—and in that sense, reality is *hypothetical*. How many times have you woken up in the morning to realize that what you perceived as real a few minutes ago was actually a dream? How many times has your *perception* of reality changed dramatically when your *understanding* of reality has shifted?

At this level of insight, the point is not to obtain a new understanding of reality; it's to recognize that *all* understandings of reality arise as hypothetical interpretations of subjective experience. As I was first cultivating this level, this really started to register for me when I recognized that even the basic building blocks of my worldview—like the existence of time, space, and multiple conscious subjects—are hypothetical interpretations of my subjective experiences.

EXPERIENCE AS MORE FUNDAMENTAL THAN REALITY

In addition to recognizing the hypothetical nature of reality, at this level of insight, you also realize that your perception of reality arises *within* your field of present-moment subjective experience. In this sense, your subjective experience itself is more fundamental than any particular understanding of reality. This is the inverse of the way we perceive things at the reality level; at that level, we perceive ourselves and our consciousness as phenomena arising *within reality*, with *reality* being more fundamental.

These two perspectives are *not* incompatible; at the reality level, you notice the real self arising within reality, while at this level, you also notice your experience of reality arising within your field of subjective experience. Experience-focused perception doesn't require your *understanding* of reality (your worldview) to change *at all*, and you don't need to *devalue* reality at this level, either. The understandings that reality is hypothetical and that experience is more fundamental than reality don't imply that nothing is real, that reality *is* subjective experience, or that your real self is alone in the universe.

What happens to the real self and the interdependent self at the presence level? We recognize them as interpreted and hypothetical, just like the rest of reality. (We don't lose the ability to say and think things like "I'm going to eat dinner now"—however, we recognize the interpreted and hypothetical nature of the "I" that we're referring to.) What happens to the witness at this level? Nothing. The witness continues witnessing subjective experience (including interpretations of subjective experience).

※❦※

To better understand the distinction between the reality level and the presence level, let's consider my sleep last night from each perspective. From the reality level perspective, I'd describe last night's sleep as follows: I lay down on my bed, got drowsy, lost consciousness for a while, regained consciousness in a dream state, lost consciousness again for a while, then regained consciousness in a waking state.

At the presence level, I retain the capacity to view last night's sleep in terms of my worldview (as described above). I also *gain* the capacity to view last night's sleep in terms of my current subjective experience: for instance, I'm aware of a current experience of having a time-ordered narrative memory of lying down, drowsiness, dreaming, and waking. I'm also aware of a current experience of thinking, "My real self must have lost consciousness at some point while sleeping last night because the time I spent dreaming seems less than the eight hours of clock time that elapsed while I was asleep."

From the reality level perspective, all your experiences—including both your dreams and your waking experiences—arise in the context of your real self (and, if you share my current worldview, that means your physical body); your real self is the context in which your subjective experiences arise, and reality is the context in which various subjects (that is, beings like you) come and go. However, from the perspective of the presence level, the contextual roles of experience and reality are inverted: *your present field of subjective experience* becomes the context in which *reality* "arises" (that is, is experienced and understood by you). Your present field of subjective experience is *your* universe; it's the fundamental context in which *all* your experiences (of various realities, dreams, your real self, other beings, and more) come and go.

PRESENCE AND IMMORTALITY

Note that my memory of last night's sleep doesn't include memories of periods of unconsciousness. If we define unconsciousness as the absence of all experience, then, by definition, unconsciousness cannot be experienced directly (though it *can* be inferred). This is in line with my memory of what I experienced last night: lying down followed by drowsiness followed by dreaming followed by waking, with no experience of intervening unconsciousness.

From the perspective of the reality level, your consciousness (that is, your subjective experience) comes and goes in reality, but reality itself is (objectively) ever-present. From the perspective of the presence level, various experiences (of dreams, various realities, and more) come and go in your field of present-moment subjective experience, but your field of experience itself is (subjectively) ever-present—meaning simply that you will never experience a complete absence of experience.

Note that there's a big difference between *subjectively* ever-present and *objectively* ever-present. If you're wondering whether your field of experience might be *objectively* ever-present (via immortality, reincarnation, and so forth), you're wondering about how consciousness fits into reality; this is a reality-level concern. There's nothing wrong with exploring reality-level concerns; however, if these concerns are worrisome to you, they're most likely related to your fear of nonexistence. When you can find joy in simply experiencing—and when questions about immortality, reincarnation, and so forth become less worrisome—you may be starting to gain the capacity to perceive at the presence level.

Notice whether you have an impulse to devalue the presence-level perspective as "just subjective" or as "less real" than the reality-level perspective; this impulse is an obstacle to entering a state of presence (and it's an obstacle to entering all the following levels of insight, as well). In my experience, devaluing subjectivity is a moral stance that frequently shows up in the culture of science. Those of us who come from a scientific background will likely have some work to do to open ourselves to presence and to let go of our attachment to viewing reality as the supreme context.

IN OTHER FRAMEWORKS

I believe the state of presence may be a key aspect of *mysticism* (in Buddhism, Christianity, and many other spiritual traditions).

Recognizing the interpreted nature of reality seems related to the concept of *deconstruction* in postmodern philosophy.

Devaluing subjectivity seems related to *scientism, scientific materialism,* and Ken Wilber's concept of *flatland.*

SUMMARY

In this chapter and the next, we explore the view, state of mind, and experiences associated with each of the seven levels of insight that I've identified. At the beginning of this exploration, we believe we're *part of* reality. After articulating what *reality* means and exploring various ways of grounding yourself *in* reality, this chapter shows how to shift your sense of self *beyond* reality. From this vantage point, it becomes possible to view subjective experience as *more fundamental* than reality; this prepares the way for transcending self (as described in the next chapter).

As I define it, *reality* is the set of phenomena perceived both by you and by others who share your worldview. Your *worldview* is a set of interrelated concepts (a frame of reference) that supports your perception of reality. Different worldviews may support the perception of vastly different phenomena. At level 1—the *reality level*—you perceive yourself to be a part of reality (whatever reality consists of for you). Your view of what's real allows you to discover important truths about life and allows you to communicate and collaborate with others who share a similar view; however, your view of reality also hides important truths—truths that don't fit within your view of what's real. Any spiritual or secular framework that either positions you as part of reality or ignores your relationship to reality is operating at this first level of insight. Reaching this level is an important accomplishment in terms of mental health and the ability to function in life; don't proceed with insight practice until you're solidly grounded in the reality level.

I refer to level 2 as the *interdependence level*. At this level, you perceive yourself *as* reality—*all of* reality. You perceive others as all of reality, too—so, at this level, you perceive all beings as one. Remember the self you perceived at the reality level (the self that was a part of reality)? Let's call that self your *real self*. Let's call the self you perceive at the interdependence level your *interdependent self*. To perceive yourself as one with reality, notice the edges of your real self, notice the arbitrariness of your choice of those edges, and consider more expansive ways of viewing yourself.

At the third level of insight, you perceive yourself as *the witness* of phenomena—that which is aware. (I refer to this as the *witnessing level*.) Although diverse phenomena arise and subside—thoughts, feelings, perceptions, worldviews, and more—awareness itself (as the witness of phenomena) is unchanged and unaffected.

At the fourth level of insight—which I call the *presence level*—our relationship to reality shifts and present-moment subjective experience assumes a much more prominent role. Cultivating this level (and all that follow) requires building the capacity to shift from *concept-focused* perception (in which your attention is mainly on conceptual experiences and you may not recognize your subjective experience *as* subjective experience) to *experience-focused* perception (in which your attention encompasses both your nonconceptual and conceptual experiences and you recognize your subjective experience *as* subjective experience).

The key understanding to cultivate at the presence level is that you never actually perceive reality directly; all you ever experience is subjective experience, and you *construct* your experience of reality as an *interpretation* of your subjective experience. In that sense, reality is *hypothetical*.

You also realize that your perception of reality arises *within* your field of present-moment subjective experience; in this sense, your subjective experience itself is more fundamental than any particular understanding of reality. This is the inverse of the way we perceive things at the reality level; at that level, we perceive ourselves and our consciousness as phenomena arising *within reality,* with *reality* being more fundamental. Your present field of subjective experience is *your* universe; it's the fundamental context in which all your experiences (of various realities, dreams, your real self, other beings, and more) come and go.

CHAPTER 13

CULTIVATE PRESENCE THROUGH MEDITATION

INSIGHT COMES MORE EASILY to some people than to others—and for a given person, some levels of insight will come more easily than others. I believe that accessing a state of presence (as described in the previous chapter) can be especially challenging. (It was certainly challenging for me, at first!) This chapter describes a number of formal meditation practices that can be helpful for cultivating presence. (Entering a state of presence is an essential prerequisite for transcending self, which is the topic of the next chapter.)

There are a couple of important prerequisites for the insight practices described in this chapter. First, build mindfulness by doing enough concentration meditation to reach at least the intermediate concentration milestones (as described in chapter 7). Next, build attentional expansiveness by meditating on your entire field of experience (as described in the section "Expanding Your Field of View" in chapter 8). With less mindfulness, you may be able to *understand* presence (conceptually), but you will have a hard time accessing a *state* of presence.

A FRAMEWORK FOR INSIGHT PRACTICE

In chapter 2, I describe a general framework for meditation; in this section, I expand that framework, providing additional suggestions specific to insight practice. The sections that follow describe specific insight practices that you can plug into this framework. When you're first learning how to do these practices, it's best to do them in formal meditation practice sessions; after you've gained some familiarity with them, you can try doing them informally (interspersed in your daily life).

PREPARING FOR INSIGHT PRACTICE

Insight practice can be challenging, and it can require a lot of resources. To get the best results from insight practice, do it when you're at your best. Plan ahead—in the twenty-four hours preceding a session of insight practice, spend some time and energy cultivating vitality.

Your *edge level* is the level of insight that's your current edge for growth; you'll spend most of your practice session cultivating the state corresponding to this level (this is your *edge state)*. Before a session of insight practice, estimate your current edge level. Make sure you understand the view, practices, and experiences associated with each level up to and including your edge level.

DOING INSIGHT PRACTICE

To begin a formal meditation session in which you want to do insight practice, start by doing some concentration meditation or another mindfulness practice. How much (and what type of) mindfulness you need depends on what level of insight you're working on; in general, the more mindfulness, the better—and for the presence level and beyond, I recommend at least an intermediate level of concentration with as much attentional expansiveness as possible.

After cultivating mindfulness at the start of your meditation session, shift to insight practice. As described in the section "Level 1: Reality" in chapter 12, you should be firmly grounded in reality as a prerequisite for insight practice. Start insight practice by entering the state corresponding to level 2, then the state corresponding to level 3, and so forth, until you get to your edge level; then spend most of your practice session focused on entering your edge state. To enter your edge state:

1. If your edge level has associated practices, do them.
2. Use the view associated with your edge level to make sense of current phenomena, and notice what you experience.
3. Compare your actual experiences with your expected experiences (the experiences associated with your edge level). (The previous two chapters of this book describe experiences associated with each level of insight). Take note of any ways in which these don't seem to match, and ask yourself how you can reconcile these differences.

If you find that your degree of mindfulness starts dropping (and you start getting distracted), shift back to concentration or another form of mindfulness practice; shift to insight practice again when your mindfulness is stronger. When you find yourself getting fatigued, take a break from meditation and restore your vitality.

If you believe you've entered your edge state, rest there and let mindfulness and insight merge; aim for a high degree of mindfulness with simultaneous and continuous insight. At first, your edge state may arise momentarily and fleetingly; once you've recognized it, recalling what it was like can help you re-enter it in future practice sessions.

REFLECTING ON INSIGHT PRACTICE

After a session of insight practice, assess what you experienced. If you're confident that you entered your edge state, set an intention to carry insight practice forward into daily life and use the experiences of daily life as further practice material. (However, be aware of the risks of overconfidence, as described in the following subsection.) If you *aren't* confident that you entered your edge state, there are a number of possible explanations, including the following:

- you may not yet have a clear enough understanding of the view, practices, or experiences associated with your edge level;
- you may be holding a belief that's incompatible with the view associated with your edge level, and that belief may be interfering with your perception; or,
- if there are specific practices associated with your edge level, you may not yet be proficient enough in them.

At this point, your task is to assess the cause of your difficulties and to decide what you intend to do next. This may not be an easy task due to the wide range of possible causes; this is why many people find it helpful to consult with spiritual mentors and teachers regularly when doing insight practice.

WORKING WITH MENTORS AND TEACHERS

In insight practice, an important function of a spiritual mentor or teacher is *pointing out* states of insight; this involves creating the conditions for states of insight to arise and helping you recognize them when they do. Pointing out can be done in dialogue with a spiritual mentor or teacher; it can also be done through published material (for instance, part 3 of this book is basically a big set of pointing out instructions).

One way to evaluate your progress in insight is to expose yourself to descriptions of insight experiences in a wide range of published material. Do these descriptions make sense to you? Do they describe experiences that seem familiar to you or experiences that seem foreign? When descriptions of insight experiences from a wide range of sources make sense to you and seem familiar, this is a good indication that you're making progress in cultivating insight.

Working with published material can make a wide range of spiritual teachings accessible to you and can help you identify teachers and mentors you resonate with; however, in general, supplementing published material with dialogue is much more effective than working with published material alone. One thing that makes working with published material tricky is the fact that terms like *spiritual awakening* and *insight* mean different things to different people; a good mentor or teacher can help you resolve this confusion. Another limitation of published material is that it can't respond to you and give you feedback.

There are two situations in which feedback from a mentor or teacher is especially important: under-confidence and overconfidence. When you're under-confident—that is, when you believe that you may have actually accessed a given insight state but you lack confidence and certainty about this assessment—no amount of reading can substitute for conversations about this with spiritual mentors and teachers you respect. When you're overconfident—that is, you *think* you've accessed a given state of insight, but actually, you *haven't*—it's even more important to be in dialogue with spiritual mentors and teachers you trust, because otherwise, you may not ever recognize your mistake.

Investigating the Nature of Experience

We're often so focused on *understanding* what we experience that we completely ignore *experience itself.* However, presence requires not only the ability to recognize experience but also the ability to rest your attention on it and clearly distinguish it from reality. Investigating the nature of experience can help you develop these abilities (which are required for subsequent levels of insight, as well).

In this practice, you focus your attention directly on subjective experience and use inquiry (a process of questioning) to investigate its nature. In doing so, you start to recognize experience more clearly and you are directly confronted with the distinction between experience and reality.

Here's an example of how this practice might unfold. You look at something and concentrate on the visual experience you're having. You silently ask yourself, "What *is* this experience?" You hold the question in mind and look more deeply into the experience. Many thoughts arise. You feel perplexed and uneasy. When you get distracted, you start over. When you get too fatigued or disturbed, you take a break. Eventually, you experience a shift toward presence. The question fades away and you begin to perceive the experience more clearly; your intellect lets go, your body relaxes, and you feel energized. Now, you let go of the question; you rest in the shift that you've experienced and you let concentration and insight merge.

This is a mindfulness practice in that it can help increase your capacity to attend to subjective experience. It's also an insight practice in that it can help you understand (and perceive) the distinction between subjective experience and reality.

Here's an outline of the practice:

1. Concentrate on an experience.
2. Use inquiry to observe it more deeply. (If you fall into dullness or distraction, start over, and if you get fatigued or disturbed, take a break. When you experience a shift toward presence, proceed to step 3.)
3. Let concentration and insight merge. (Let go of inquiry and rest in the shift you've experienced.)

I describe these steps in detail in the following three subsections.

CONCENTRATING ON AN EXPERIENCE

Choose a current subjective experience to work with. Any experience that you can concentrate on will work—but to start with, choose an experience that's not too fleeting; it should be ongoing (or at least recurring), and it should be easy for you to concentrate on. I suggest you start with the visual experience of something you see in front of you with your eyes open; for instance, the visual experience of a stone on the floor in front of you.

Rest your attention on the experience that you've chosen. Do some concentration meditation, using the experience that you've chosen as your object of attention. If you don't have much experience with this practice, for best results, don't move on until you are in a state of at least intermediate concentration (that is, at least at the fifth milestone—the higher your level of concentration, the better). At lower levels of concentration, your attention is likely to be carried away into involuntary thinking when you get to the next step.

INVESTIGATING THE NATURE OF THE EXPERIENCE

Choose a question to help you observe the experience. There are many possible questions you could work with; I suggest you start with the question, "What *is* this?"

As you continue to concentrate on the experience, silently ask the question you've chosen. Let the question direct your attention more deeply into the experience. Observe *the experience itself.* For instance, let's say you've chosen to observe the visual experience of a stone on the floor in front of you. The goal here isn't to observe *the stone;* it's to observe *your visual experience of* the stone. Don't make this more complicated than it needs to be; if you've chosen an ongoing experience that's easy for you to concentrate on, the experience will be obvious and glaring—*right there.* You can't miss it.

Continue to concentrate on the experience as you hold the question and mindfully attend to what arises in response. Simply observe—don't seek explanations or rational understanding. This practice isn't a scientific or philosophical endeavor. For instance, investigating correlations between the experience and other phenomena (like neural activity) may be interesting and may have useful applications, but it's not a part of this practice. Simply allow the question you're asking to draw your attention more deeply into the experience. Allow thoughts, emotions, and body sensations to arise; don't try to stop them, but don't get distracted by them, either. Eventually, you may reach a state in which no more words arise. That's fine; continue to hold the question and observe the experience more deeply.

Eventually (usually within seconds or minutes) one of the following things is likely to happen:

- **You may fall into dullness or distraction.** If you're not too fatigued or disturbed, return to the previous step (concentrating on an experience without asking any questions) to restore your concentration—then proceed on to this step (using inquiry) and try again. (You can choose a different experience and/or a different question to work with if you want.)
- **You may get fatigued.** If so, it's time to take a break from insight practice and restore your vitality. This practice is best approached in brief sessions of high intensity—not marathon sessions.
- **You may feel disturbed and overwhelmed.** If so, it's time to take a break. (For important cautions about insight practice, see the section "Risks of Insight Practice" in chapter 11.)
- **You may experience a shift toward presence.** The question fades away and you begin to perceive the experience more clearly. Your intellect lets go, your body relaxes, and you feel energized. It may take a while before this shift occurs, but when it does, it may occur fairly suddenly. This shift may be subtle—especially at first—so don't necessarily expect fireworks.

Don't expect to get a clear, comfortable answer to your question, even when you experience a shift toward presence. (Changes in conceptual understanding may accompany insight, but insight is distinct from conceptual understanding.)

LETTING CONCENTRATION AND INSIGHT MERGE

After you experience a shift toward presence, let go of the question you've been asking. Rest in the shift that you've experienced and let concentration and insight merge. Aim for a stable, clear state of mind in which you can rest in the recognition of your subjective experience. (If you want, you can return your focus to concentration practice at this point; you may find that insight makes concentration practice easier.)

When insight and/or concentration fade, you can start this practice over again (possibly choosing a different experience and/or a different question to work with). When you're ready to end your practice session, set an intention to carry the benefits of the practice into your daily life.

CHOOSING AND ASKING QUESTIONS

You can vary the basic practice above by choosing different questions to use in your investigation and by choosing different types of experiences to investigate. The fact that there are so many possible combinations of questions and experiences can make this an exceptionally rich and varied practice.

When choosing a question, any question can work if it helps you observe the experience more deeply and recognize its relationship to reality. Here are some of my favorites:

- "What *is* this experience?"
- "Where *is* this experience?"
- "How *big* is this experience?"
- "What *shape* is this experience?"

- "What *color* is this experience?"
- "Where was this experience before I experienced it?"
- "Where does this experience go after I experience it?"
- "Can this experience be damaged?"
- "What's the difference between this experience and reality?"

It's fine to make up your own questions. Ask questions the help you observe *the experience itself.* (For instance, if you're observing the visual experience of a stone, your questions should be about the visual experience—not about the stone. Asking "What kind of stone is it?" won't help you cultivate insight.)

It's okay to ask a variety of questions about a given experience, but spend some time with each question. Don't move on to another question just because an answer arose. In particular, be suspicious of any answer that you feel especially certain of. Continue to hold the question and observe more deeply.

Some questions may seem to have simple answers, while some may not seem to have *any* answer. Some questions may seem very confusing. All of this is okay; the point is to let the question lead you to a deeper appreciation of the experience. (If the question you're working with isn't doing that, it's time to move on to another question.)

Don't try to stop answers from arising; answers aren't harmful, as long as you don't get distracted by them. But keep in mind that insight is your goal, not answers—and the answers aren't the insight. (Insight is a shift in perception, not just a shift in understanding.)

BUILDING RANGE AND EXPANSIVENESS

After you get used to doing this practice with a visual experience, branch out and explore what this practice is like with as many other types of experiences as possible. Work with a variety of other sensory experiences, including sounds (like the sound of recorded music playing), tactile and body sensations, smells, and tastes. Try working with the kinesthetic and energetic experiences of breathing and with the sign. Try working with something you imagine or remember. It's much easier to work with nonconceptual experiences, so start there—but, with enough mindfulness and concentration, you can do this practice with conceptual experiences, too.

Regardless of the experience you choose, note that you must be able to concentrate on it with at least an intermediate level of concentration before you can use it as a basis for this practice. Before you try this practice with an unfamiliar type of experience, do some concentration meditation in which you take that type of experience as your object of attention.

After you can do this practice with a wide range of experiences, start doing it with successively more expansive fields of experience. You might start this process by working with two sensory modalities simultaneously. Later, try working with your entire field of subjective experience. You can even try working with the referent of the concept "everything you ever have experienced or will experience!" In my experience, this practice becomes more powerful as you choose more expansive fields of experience to work with.

INVESTIGATING YOUR EXPERIENCE OF REALITY

Reality is the set of phenomena that can be perceived both by you and by others who share your worldview. We tend to forget about subjective experience and assume we perceive reality directly. In the practice described in this section, you challenge this assumption by using inquiry to investigate your experience of reality; in the process, you discover ways in which reality is more ephemeral than subjective experience.

Before trying this practice, gain familiarity with the practice described in the previous section (investigating the nature of experience). Like that practice, investigating your experience of reality can support your ability to recognize experience, rest your attention on it, and clearly distinguish it from reality—abilities that are required for accessing a state of presence.

Here's an example of how this practice might unfold. You look at something—for instance, a stone. You concentrate on the visual experience you're having. You notice your sense that this experience corresponds to an actual, *real* stone. You use questions to investigate the relationship between the visual experience you're having and the supposed reality of the stone; for instance, "What do I experience more directly: experience or reality? If this is an experience, where is reality? What *is* reality? Could I ever experience reality directly? Am I sure this is real?" Many thoughts may arise. You may feel perplexed and uneasy. When you get distracted, you start over. When you get too fatigued or disturbed, you take a break. Eventually, you experience a shift toward presence. Your intellect lets go, your body relaxes, and you feel energized. You begin to perceive the experience itself more clearly and vividly, and the reality that supposedly corresponds to the experience starts to seem more ephemeral. You rest in the shift you've experienced and let concentration and insight merge.

Here's an outline of the practice:

1. Concentrate on an experience of something that seems real.
2. Use inquiry to investigate the relationship between the experience and reality. (If you fall into dullness or distraction, start over, and if you get fatigued or disturbed, take a break. When you experience a shift toward presence, proceed to step 3.)
3. Let concentration and insight merge. (Let go of inquiry and rest in the shift you've experienced.)

I describe these steps in detail in the following three subsections.

CONCENTRATING ON AN EXPERIENCE

Choose something that seems real. Focus your attention on your current subjective experience of this thing. The experience shouldn't be too fleeting; it should be ongoing (or, at least, recurring), and it should be easy for you to concentrate on. I suggest you start with the visual experience of something you see in front of you with your eyes open; for instance, the visual experience of a stone on the floor in front of you.

Rest your attention on the experience. Do some concentration meditation, using the experience as your object of attention. If this practice is new to you, for best results, don't move on until you're in a state of at least intermediate concentration (that is, at least at the fifth milestone); the higher your level of concentration, the better. (After you gain some familiarity with this practice, it can be effective at lower levels of concentration, as well.)

INVESTIGATING THE CORRESPONDING REALITY

Notice your sense that this experience corresponds to something real. As you continue to concentrate on the experience you've chosen, silently ask yourself questions to help you investigate the relationship between the experience and the supposed reality that corresponds to it. There are many possible questions you could work with; I suggest you start with the questions, "What do I experience more directly: experience or reality?" and "If this is an experience, where is reality?" Ask your questions one at a time and mindfully attend to what arises in response. Allow thoughts, emotions, and body sensations to arise; don't try to stop them, but don't get distracted by them, either.

Eventually (usually within seconds or minutes) one of the following things is likely to happen:

- **You may fall into dullness or distraction.** If you're not too fatigued or disturbed, return to the previous step (concentrat-

ing on the experience without asking any questions) to restore your concentration—then proceed on to this step (using inquiry) and try again. (You can choose a different
experience and/or different questions to work with if you
want.)

- **You may get fatigued.** If so, it's time to take a break from insight practice and restore your vitality. This practice is best
  approached in brief sessions of high intensity—not marathon
  sessions.
- **You may feel disturbed and overwhelmed.** If so, it's time to
  take a break. (For important cautions about insight practice,
  see the section "Risks of Insight Practice" in chapter 11.)
- **You may experience a shift toward presence.** You begin to
  perceive the experience itself more clearly and vividly, and the
  reality that supposedly corresponds to the experience starts to
  seem more ephemeral. You experience more humility and
  equanimity as your intellect lets go of its quest for certainty
  about what's real. Your body relaxes, and you feel energized.
  It may take a while before this shift occurs, but when it does,
  it may occur fairly suddenly. This shift may be subtle—especially at first—so don't necessarily expect fireworks.

What this practice reveals is that we don't experience reality directly; all we *ever* experience is subjective experience, and our understanding of what's real is based on our *interpretation* of our
subjective experience. In other words, reality isn't experienced; it's
interpreted. It's possible to understand this *conceptually* without doing any meditation or inquiry; however, conceptual understanding
alone is unlikely to foster ongoing shifts in *perception.* That's why
practice is important. (Note: I find *reality* to be a useful concept,
and I find it helpful to distinguish what's real from what's not. Losing the ability to make that distinction isn't awakening, it's psychosis; becoming psychotic is *not* the aim of this practice.)

LETTING CONCENTRATION AND INSIGHT MERGE

After you experience a shift toward presence, let go of your questions. Rest in the shift that you've experienced and let concentration and insight merge. Aim for a stable, clear state of mind with continued humility and equanimity. (If you want, you can return your focus to concentration practice at this point; you may find that insight makes concentration practice easier.)

When insight and/or concentration fade, you can start this practice over again (possibly choosing different questions and/or a different experience to work with). When you're ready to end your practice session, set an intention to carry the benefits of the practice into your daily life.

CHOOSING AND ASKING QUESTIONS

You can vary the basic practice above by choosing different questions to use in your investigation and by choosing different types of experiences to investigate. When choosing a question, choose any question that helps you investigate the relationship between the experience and the supposed reality that corresponds to it. Here are some of my favorites:

- "What do I experience more directly: experience or reality?"
- "If this is an experience, where is reality?"
- "What *is* reality?"
- "Could I ever experience reality directly?"
- "Am I sure this is real?"
- "Is the reality of this thing a *fact* or an *interpretation of my experience?* If it's an interpretation, are there other possible interpretations?"
- "Could this be a dream?"

It's fine to make up your own questions. What are you curious about? Go there!

CHOOSING EXPERIENCES TO INVESTIGATE

You can up the ante in this practice by working with multisensory experiences. For instance, instead of just looking at a rock, look at it while simultaneously holding it in your hand and feeling its solidity. Instead of just looking at a raisin, put it in your mouth, feel its texture, and taste it. Concentrate on the total sensory experience, then investigate the relationship between that experience and reality.

IN OTHER FRAMEWORKS

You may be familiar with materialism and related frameworks, which devalue subjective experience as a mere byproduct (or epiphenomenon) of reality. In my experience, doing this practice can shift that orientation; through this practice, subjective experience gains prominence as the experience of reality is seen to arise *within* subjective experience as a *subset* of subjective experience. (Notice that this increased prominence of subjective experience doesn't imply that the universe is in your head, that you're alone in the universe, or anything else about the *structure* of reality; while this practice reveals reality as *interpreted,* it doesn't privilege *any particular* interpretation.)

CULTIVATING EXPERIENCE-FOCUSED PERCEPTION

Accessing presence involves cultivating a new way of perceiving phenomena: experience-focused perception. Alternating between concept-focused and experience-focused perception can be a helpful practice for distinguishing these modes of perception and for building your capacity to enter a state of experience-focused perception at will. The following are the steps in this practice:

1. First, invoke concept-focused perception by focusing on objects in reality (for instance, nearby tables and chairs). Notice how you seem to be looking *right at* reality.

2. Now, to switch to experience-focused perception, notice the subjective experiences associated with what you're looking at. Notice how what you're looking at is *nothing other than* subjective experience. Now, you don't see reality at all; you just see subjective experience. Where did reality go?

3. Now, try to see both subjective experience and reality at the same time. For me, when I try to do this, I imagine a ghostly reality that somehow corresponds to my subjective experience. Where is this reality? The subjective experience is clearly right there, but I don't know where reality is.

4. Now, switch back to concept-focused perception. Forget about subjective experience and just notice reality again. Notice how your perception loses some vividness as you return to perceiving subjective experience as just a means to an end (if you perceive it at all). Notice the magic trick that you do to perceive reality: concept-focused perception automatically takes your worldview and uses it to translate subjective experience into a conceptual understanding of reality—automatically, involuntarily and unconsciously.

I suggest you practice switching between concept-focused and experience-focused perception until you can do so at will.

VISUALIZING YOUR INTERPRETATIONS OF EXPERIENCE

Accessing presence involves cultivating experience-focused perception. Visualizing our conceptual interpretations of experience can help us stay grounded in experience-focused perception and can help us recognize our frames of reference; recognizing our frames of reference is also helpful in the no-reference level of insight (as described in the section "Level 7: No Reference" in chapter 14).

WHAT WE LOSE IN CONCEPT-FOCUSED PERCEPTION

Our mind is constantly at work using our worldview to interpret nonconceptual experiences and generate conceptual experiences; these conceptual experiences arise in our awareness as conceptual knowledge. Normally, in concept-focused perception, we don't recognize these conceptual experiences as interpretations or even as *experiences;* for instance, we look at a candle and we simply *know* that it's a candle.

The automatic, unconscious, involuntary nature of this interpretive process is very fast and efficient, but a lot gets lost in the process: awareness of the original nonconceptual visual experience corresponding to the candle, awareness of the knowledge arising, and awareness of the *interpreted nature* of that knowledge. When we're entrenched in concept-focused perception, most or all of our attention is on knowledge; almost none is on our experiences. (This is why experiences seem dull—lacking in vividness—in concept-focused perception.)

RECOGNIZING CONCEPTUAL EXPERIENCES

In experience-focused perception, it's still possible to interpret the meaning of your subjective experiences in terms of your worldview. You look at a candle and you *know* that it's a candle; that knowledge arises as a conceptual experience. If you recognize the experience (of knowing that it's a candle) *as* a conceptual experience (that's arising based on your interpretation of your nonconceptual experience), you get a bit more grounded in experience-focused perception; otherwise, you've taken a step back toward concept-focused perception.

This is analogous to recognizing thoughts in concentration meditation: if you can recognize a thought *as* a thought (that is, if you can recognize the *experience* of having the thought), the thought doesn't impede your concentration. If you don't recognize the thought as a thought (and your attention instead goes to what the thought refers to), you're likely to be drawn into thinking.

VISUALIZING CONCEPTUAL INTERPRETATIONS

Experience-focused perception requires relating phenomena to *experience*. To stay grounded in experience-focused perception, I find it helpful to find ways to become more aware of the conceptual experiences that underlie my knowledge of reality. One way I do this is to visualize a conceptual overlay on my nonconceptual subjective experiences.

To try this, look around the room and notice your mind using concepts to understand your nonconceptual subjective experiences. As you notice this, visualize the concepts as tags. For instance, when you look at a candle, imagine the word "candle" floating next to the candle. When you look down a hallway, imagine a grid overlaid on the hallway; the grid makes your perception of space explicit by marking off distance. When you remember something that happened a while ago, imagine it tagged with a rough date and time.

Isn't it amazing that all of this normally happens automatically and unconsciously? Visualizing the conceptual output of the process of conceptual understanding is one way to make this process more explicit. (This can be viewed as a form of noting.) You are identifying the *conceptual* subjective experiences that get automatically created based on your *nonconceptual* subjective experiences.

Of course, you're not going to be able to visualize *all* your interpretations—and that's okay. Even visualizing a small subset of your interpretations can help remind you of the interpreted nature of your perception of reality (thus helping you stay grounded in experience-focused perception).

SUMMARY

Accessing presence can be challenging; this chapter describes a number of formal meditation practices that can be helpful for cultivating presence. (Presence is an essential prerequisite for transcending self, which is the topic of the next chapter.)

In chapter 2, I describe a general framework for meditation; in this chapter, I expand that framework, providing additional suggestions specific to insight practice.

There are a couple of important prerequisites for the insight practices described in this chapter. First, build mindfulness by doing enough concentration meditation to reach at least the intermediate concentration milestones. Next, build attentional expansiveness by meditating on your entire field of experience. With less mindfulness, you may be able to *understand* presence (conceptually), but you will have a hard time accessing a *state* of presence.

In insight practice, an important function of a spiritual mentor or teacher is pointing out states of insight; this involves creating the conditions for states of insight to arise and helping you recognize them when they do.

We're often so focused on *understanding* what we experience that we completely ignore *experience itself.* However, presence requires not only the ability to recognize experience but also the ability to rest your attention on it and clearly distinguish it from reality. Investigating the nature of experience can help you develop these abilities. In this practice, you focus your attention directly on subjective experience and use inquiry (a process of questioning) to investigate its nature.

We tend to forget about subjective experience and assume we perceive reality directly. You can challenge this assumption by using inquiry to investigate your experience of reality; in the process, you discover ways in which reality is more ephemeral than subjective experience.

Accessing presence involves cultivating a new way of perceiving phenomena: experience-focused perception. Alternating between concept-focused and experience-focused perception can be a helpful practice for distinguishing these modes of perception and for building your capacity to enter a state of experience-focused perception at will.

Visualizing your conceptual interpretations of experience can help you stay grounded in experience-focused perception and can help you recognize your frames of reference.

CHAPTER 14

TRANSCEND SELF

ONCE YOU CAN ENTER a state of presence, you're ready to start cultivating the next two levels of insight (described in the next two sections), in which you will further transform your understanding and perception of self. Then, in the last section of this chapter, you will return your attention to the real self and address some problems that often arise in relation to spiritual frameworks (like this one).

LEVEL 5: EVENNESS

At the reality level, we consider ourselves to be real—but, as we saw at the witnessing level, at a deeper level, we perceive ourselves to be that which is aware (the witness). The fifth level of insight unfolds as we try to examine the witness more closely. (I call this fifth level the *evenness level,* for reasons that will soon become clear.)

SEEKING THE ELUSIVE WITNESS

At this level, we recognize that in a state of experience-focused perception, no matter how long and hard we search for the witness, we'll never find it. To understand what this means, let's compare the witness to the real self. It's not hard to find the real self; in fact, experiences of the real self are hard to avoid. What you consider the real self to *be* depends on your worldview—but if your worldview is similar to mine, the visual experience of your body in the mirror, the sound of your voice, and your body sensations are all nonconceptual experiences of the real self. The concept of the *real self* is *grounded in nonconceptual experience* in that it refers to a specific pattern of nonconceptual experiences. When we recognize that pattern, we say, "That's me!"

The unusual thing about the witness is that you can search your field of nonconceptual experience forever, and you will *never* find a nonconceptual experience of the witness. We've defined the witness as an entity *distinct from experience* that *does the experiencing.* That means that no matter what nonconceptual experience we turn our attention to, we will always perceive that experience to be "not-witness;" it always seems that the witness must be something else.

Of course, we *can* have *conceptual* experiences of the witness—we can think about it and talk about it all day if we want. But we will never experience it nonconceptually (in the way that we experience the real self). We will never see it, hear it, or taste it. The witness is a concept without a nonconceptual referent—it's not grounded in nonconceptual experience.

What about your convincing, ongoing sense that the witness exists somewhere specific in reality? (For instance, I tend to have the sense that the witness sits somewhere in the middle of my head.) This is an artifact of concept-focused perception that disappears when you switch to experience-focused perception. Whatever the experience is that you associate with the witness, when you turn your attention to that experience, you will recognize that *it's just an experience.* It won't feel like the witness at all (even if it felt like the witness before, in concept-focused perception).

Some things are much easier to try than they are to explain, and this is one of them. So, try the following practice. Notice where you believe the witness sits in reality. (Perhaps it's in the middle of your head.) Pay attention to reality (invoking concept-focused perception), and you will have a convincing perception that *that's* where the witness is sitting. Now, focus your attention on that spot or area and notice the sensations that you *actually* experience there, as well as any and all nonconceptual experiences that you've been associating with the witness (invoking experience-focused perception). What happens? Whatever it is that you've been experiencing, it no longer feels like the witness. In fact, your perception of the witness probably disappears, leaving no trace. If the witness seems to move somewhere else, follow it and repeat the experiment; you will get the same results each time. (The section "Investigating Your Experience of Self" in the following section describes a similar meditation practice in detail.)

Does the real self (or some part of it) do the witnessing? In concept-focused perception, this might make sense—it depends on your worldview. (Personally, my worldview includes conscious beings inhabiting physical bodies and witnessing their experiences. Does that worldview make sense? Maybe not, but it's the best one I've got!) Recall that in the previous chapter, we learned that the real self is a hypothetical, conceptual interpretation of experience— just like everything in reality. As part of that conceptual interpretation, you may believe that the real self (or some part of it) does the witnessing; however, notice that holding this belief is different than finding a nonconceptual experience of the witness in your field of experience. You may believe that the real self is doing the witnessing, and you may have nonconceptual experiences that correspond to the real self; however, when you examine those nonconceptual experiences in a state of experience-focused perception, you always perceive them to be "not-witness," just like all other experiences; it always seems that the witness must be something else. Try it and you'll see what I mean.

THE UNITY OF AWARENESS AND EXPERIENCE

In experience-focused perception, the witness—that which is aware —can't be found. But clearly, you're aware of your experiences. What's going on? The answer is quite simple. Awareness and experience are two sides of the same coin; you can't have one without the other. The concept of the witness takes awareness *out of* experience and locates it in a hypothetical observer (the witness). After you recognize that the witness can't be found, the perceptual practice of this level of insight is to *let go of* the concept of the witness and recognize awareness as an integral aspect of *all* experience.

There are at least a couple ways to do this. You can conceive of awareness as an inseparable aspect of experience, in which case your experiences seem to "glow" with awareness—this glow is the *luminosity of experience.* (If experience didn't glow, you wouldn't be able to "see" it.) Conversely, you can conceive of experience as an inseparable aspect of awareness, in which case your awareness seems like a space filled with your experiences—the *space of awareness* (which is equivalent to your *field of experience).*

Either way you conceive of it, at this level, the absence of a witness lends a quality of *evenness* to experience and awareness. Your awareness is present in *all* your experiences (as opposed to concentrated in a separate witness) and everywhere there is awareness, there is experience (your space of awareness is always completely filled with your experiences); experience and awareness always arise together. (What about awareness of awareness itself? If you're aware of it, then by definition, it's an experience—in this case, the experience of awareness.) To the extent that you identify with awareness, you may feel as if you are one with all your experiences at this level.

In Other Frameworks

The concept of *the unity of awareness and experience* seems related to various flavors of nondualism in spiritual thought.

Searching for the witness (and not finding it) seems related to the Buddhist concept of *anatta* or *anatman* ("non-self").

If one conceives of awareness/experience (as perceived at this level of insight) as divine, and reality (as perceived in concept-focused perception) as non-divine, the conceptual framework that corresponds to this level could be viewed as a form of *panentheism.*

INVESTIGATING YOUR EXPERIENCE OF SELF

We usually take it for granted that we're somewhere "in here," experiencing things "out there." Challenging this assumption through inquiry can be an effective way of cultivating the evenness level of insight (described in the previous section). I call this practice *investigating your experience of self*. In this section, I describe this practice in depth. (This is an insight practice. Before trying this practice, see "A Framework for Insight Practice" and "Investigating the Nature of Experience" in the previous chapter.)

Here's an example of how this practice might unfold. You look at something. You concentrate on the visual experience you're having. You notice your sense of being a witness of the experience, separate from the experience. As you concentrate on the experience, you silently ask yourself, "What experiences this?" and you start searching for a direct experience of the supposed witness. When you get distracted, you start over. When you get too fatigued or disturbed, you take a break. Eventually, you experience a shift toward evenness: your intellect lets go, your body relaxes, you feel energized, and you perceive a newfound evenness in your field of subjective experience—it's clear that it's all just experience, with no separate witness to be found. You rest in the shift you've experienced and you let concentration and insight merge.

Here's an outline of the practice:

1. Concentrate on an experience.
2. Search for a separate subject (that experiences it). (If you fall into dullness or distraction, start over. If you get fatigued or disturbed, take a break. If you experience a shift toward evenness, proceed to step 3.)
3. Let concentration and insight merge. (Stop searching and rest in the shift you've experienced.)

I describe these steps in detail in the following three subsections.

CONCENTRATING ON AN EXPERIENCE

Choose a current subjective experience to work with. For this practice, the best experience to work with is your *entire field* of subjective experience (as described in the section "Expanding Your Field of View" in chapter 8). However, any experience that you can concentrate on will also work. To start with, choose an experience that's not too fleeting; it should be ongoing (or, at least, recurring), and it should be easy for you to concentrate on. If you have trouble concentrating on your entire field of experience, you might start with the visual experience of something you see in front of you with your eyes open; for instance, the visual experience of a stone on the floor in front of you.

Rest your attention on the experience that you've chosen. Do some concentration meditation, using the experience that you've chosen as your object of attention. If you don't have much experience with this practice, for best results, don't move on until you are in a state of at least intermediate concentration (that is, at least at the fifth milestone—the higher your level of concentration, the better). (After you gain some familiarity with this practice, it can be effective at lower levels of concentration, as well.)

SEARCHING FOR A SEPARATE SUBJECT

Notice your sense of being a *separate subject*—a witness or observer of the experience, distinct from the experience. As you continue to concentrate on the experience you've chosen, silently ask yourself, "What experiences this?" and start searching your field of current nonconceptual experience for this supposed separate subject. (You will need to split your attention—resting some of your attention on the experience you've chosen and using some of your attention to search for that which experiences it.)

Remember, you're searching for a *nonconceptual* experience of the supposed separate subject; you're not searching for ideas, theories, or beliefs about it. When thoughts arise (like "my body experiences this" or "my brain experiences this"), note them and move on. (One reason you may need at least an intermediate level of concentration to do this practice is that at lower levels of concentration, your attention is likely to be carried away into involuntary thinking when you start searching.)

You may have a sense that there's a location where the separate subject resides. (For me, it seems to be somewhere in my head behind my eyes.) Search there and notice what experiences you find. (For me, it's usually a subtle feeling of fullness or tension.) Regardless of what you find, ask yourself, "Have I found *what experiences*, or just another experience?"

You may wonder whether what you seek lies beyond the range of you can currently perceive. If so, *imagine* finding it, and ask yourself, "If I were to find what I'm seeking, how would I know? How would *that experience* differ from any other?" (Would it be extra-sparkly? Would it sound like monks chanting?)

As you search for the supposed separate subject, you may have fleeting experiences of something that disappears or moves elsewhere when you try to focus on it. That's fine; you don't have to *concentrate* on these experiences, you just have to *notice* them. When you notice them, remember them, and ask yourself the questions in the paragraphs above.

Don't expect to *find* what you're searching for, but *do* search. Searching helps facilitate a shift in *perception* (as opposed to a shift in conceptual understanding alone). As you search, eventually (usually within seconds or minutes) one of the following things is likely to happen:

- **You may fall into dullness or distraction.** If you're not too fatigued or disturbed, return to the previous step (concentrating on an experience without searching) to restore your concentration—then proceed on to this step (searching for that which experiences) and try again. (You can choose a different experience to work with if you want.)

- **You may get fatigued.** If so, it's time to take a break from insight practice and restore your vitality. This practice is best approached in brief sessions of high intensity—not marathon sessions.
- **You may feel disturbed and overwhelmed.** If so, it's time to take a break. (For important cautions about insight practice, see the section "Risks of Insight Practice" in chapter 11.)
- **You may experience a shift toward evenness.** You perceive a newfound *evenness* in your field of subjective experience—it's clear that it's all just experience, with no distinct subject to be found. Your intellect lets go, your body relaxes, and you feel energized. It may take a while before this shift occurs, but when it does, it may occur fairly suddenly. This shift may be subtle—especially at first—so don't necessarily expect fireworks.

LETTING CONCENTRATION AND INSIGHT MERGE

After you experience a shift toward evenness, let go of all questions and stop searching. Rest in the shift that you've experienced and let concentration and insight merge. Aim for a stable, clear state of mind with an evenness of experience. (If you want, you can return your focus to concentration practice at this point; you may find that insight makes concentration practice easier.)

When insight and/or concentration fade, you can start this practice over again (possibly choosing a different experience to work with). When you're ready to end your practice session, set an intention to carry the benefits of the practice into your daily life.

INVESTIGATING BOTH EXPERIENCE AND SELF

You can intensify the basic practice above in a couple of ways. You may have noticed the congruence between this practice and the practice of investigating the nature of experience (which is described in the previous chapter in the section "Investigating the Nature of Experience"); step one is the same in each practice, and steps two and three are similar. After you gain familiarity with each practice, you can try combining them. For instance, in step two, you might alternate between asking yourself "What *is* this?" and "What *experiences* this?" Another way to intensify this practice is to expand the field of view that you use as a starting point for the practice (as described in the section "Expanding Your Field of View" in chapter 8).

LEVEL 6: EXPERIENCE ONLY

So far, we've chased our identity (the self) from the real self into the witness, then from the witness into experience (as luminosity, the awareness aspect of experience). In the sixth level of insight, we go a step further and let go of the distinction between awareness and experience—effectively *doing away with* the last vestige of a sense of awareness/self as something distinct from experience. (I call this the *experience-only level*.)

If awareness and experience are two sides of the same coin, then why use two words to describe the same thing? The concept of *awareness* loses its meaning if it doesn't distinguish anything in particular. So, try just dropping it. What's that like? All that's left is experience. There's neither awareness nor absence of awareness; just experience arising. What happens to the luminosity of experience (that we perceived in the previous level)? At this level, experience becomes neither luminous nor non-luminous; it just *is*.

(Of course, it would be semantically equivalent to drop the concept of *experience*, leaving us only with *awareness*—and I imagine that some authors/teachers choose to do exactly that when describing conceptual frameworks that are congruent to this level. I imagine this has led to many interminable arguments between those who prefer the term *awareness* and those who prefer the term *expe-*

rience. Personally, I find it more challenging and useful to drop the concept of *awareness.*)

In the state corresponding to this level, our experience of life is simply that of subjective experience arising, with no self to be found anywhere—not as the witness, nor as awareness. (Experiences of the real self and the interdependent self continue to arise at this level, but—as in levels 4 and 5—we recognize them as interpreted and hypothetical.)

IN OTHER FRAMEWORKS

To me, the experience-only level seems even more nondual (or less dual) than the evenness level.

A view focused more on experience (and less on awareness) seems characteristic of the vipassana (or vipasyana) (often translated as "insight") practices that I've encountered in Theravada Buddhism.

LEVEL 7: NO REFERENCE

A *frame of reference* (or *framework)* is a set of interrelated concepts that allows you to make sense of experience. For instance:

- Your worldview is a frame of reference that supports your perception of reality.
- Each level of insight has an associated view, and each of these views is a frame of reference that supports entering the perceptual state associated with that level. (Even the minimal view of the experience-only level—focused on the concept of *experience*—is still a frame of reference.)
- My model of insight (as a series of levels) is a frame of reference that guides the cultivation of insight.
- My model of awakening is a frame of reference that guides the cultivation of awakening.

The levels of insight that I've identified successively refactor our foundational frame of reference, focusing our attention on increasingly simple frameworks. At the reality level, we identify with the real self (as it exists in all the complexity of reality). At the interdependence level, noticing the arbitrariness of our definition of *the real self* allows us to identify with the unity and interdependence of *all* aspects of reality. At the witnessing level, identifying with an aware witness allows us to start shifting our attention *away* from reality. At the presence level, noticing the interpreted nature of reality allows us to complete this process, shifting our attention from reality to *experience*. At the evenness level, we factor out *the witness* as an unnecessary concept, which allows us to recognize the unity of awareness and experience. At the experience-only level, we further factor out *awareness* as another unnecessary concept, which just leaves us with experience. Our foundational frame of reference can't get any simpler—or, can it?

In the seventh level of insight, which I call the *no-reference level*, we learn to recognize how frames of reference affect our perception and we realize that *no* frame of reference—not the frame of reference of the experience-only level, nor any other—can be rationally determined to be ultimate (that is, "the best"). This deals a death blow to the misconception that we can be fundamentally rational beings and opens the door to a new way of living life in which we consciously integrate intellect and intuition. This can lead to a new level of effectiveness in living life.

GRASPING ONTO YOUR SPIRITUAL PATH

After we've exhaustively chased down the self (via insight levels 1 through 6), your self appears to run and hide in the last place we would expect: *your spiritual path!* This manifests as grasping on to the frames of reference associated with your path. The symptom of this is that you view your path as "the truth," you feel threatened by competing views, and you start zealously protecting and promoting your path.

How is grasping even possible when we've obliterated all trace of self from our frame of reference? Grasping is an issue that affects the *real self*—not the witness (at the witnessing level) or the awareness that's unified with experience (at the evenness level). Wouldn't it be nice if removing the witness and awareness from our frame of reference would resolve grasping and all other problematic qualities of the real self? Unfortunately, that's not how it works. The real self is a set of patterns (or habits); changing habits generally requires a lot of hard work. If someone implies that they are perfect (that is, their real self is perfect) simply because they have achieved insight, watch out! Our propensity for grasping onto frames of reference has been lurking in the *real self* all along; in this level, we address this issue.

If insight doesn't automatically perfect the real self, what's it good for? Insight can be viewed as a process of successively shedding unfounded assumptions about ourselves and reality and learning to perceive life more clearly. If you value truth and clarity, as I do, insight practice is a way of embodying these values. Even though insight doesn't automatically perfect the real self, the clarity of insight can dramatically decrease our fear of nonexistence and can make the hard work of personal growth and healing much easier and more efficient.

HOW WE BECOME EMBEDDED IN FRAMES OF REFERENCE

You're *embedded* in a frame of reference when you experience your frame of reference as "the best" and alternative frames of reference as inferior or threatening; this makes it difficult or impossible for you to use alternative frames of reference to make sense of experience. You may not be aware of the concept of *frames of reference;* you may simply experience the frame of reference in which you are embedded as "the truth" or "the way things are" and other frames of reference as ridiculous or incorrect. If you even consider alternative frames of reference (with competing concepts), you do so by shrinking them down to what can be understood in terms of your preferred framework.

The more we *value* a particular framework, the easier it is for us to become embedded in it. All spiritual practices are supported by some framework (whether explicit or implicit); we often value our spiritual practices highly, so it's easy to become embedded in their associated frameworks. If you find a particular spiritual path helpful, you're likely to start incorporating its frame of reference into your worldview; then, to the extent that you're embedded in your worldview, you are likely to find yourself zealously protecting and promoting your spiritual path and its associated conceptual frameworks.

DISEMBEDDING YOURSELF FROM FRAMES OF REFERENCE

You can disembed yourself from frames of reference by understanding them, learning to recognize them, and becoming aware of how they affect your perception. Here are some practices for cultivating this capacity:

1. **Learn to *recognize* how you make sense of life.** Learn to recognize frames of reference. Recognize how they act both as lenses (focusing attention on some aspects of experience) and filters (hiding other aspects).

2. **Investigate your *experience* of making sense of life.** Your subjective experience is transformed into conceptual knowledge via a frame of reference; I call this process *conceptual understanding*. For instance, when you look at a tree, conceptual understanding is how you *know* that it's a tree. Thinking is the process by which a frame of reference is refined and elaborated upon. Conceptual understanding and thinking are ordinarily automatic, involuntary, and unconscious, but you can learn to become conscious of them. Do so, then meditate on your *subjective experiences* of conceptual understanding and thinking. For instance, become aware of your

thoughts *themselves*—not just what you're thinking *about.* (You started developing this capacity in the presence level when you learned to shift from concept-focused to experience-focused perception.) Watch your conceptual understanding of life unfold before your eyes. Notice the frames of reference that underlie your conceptual understandings and recognize that every conceptual understanding depends entirely on some frame of reference.

3. **Stop seeking the ultimate frame of reference.** Recognize that no frame of reference (and, therefore, no belief system or conceptual model) can be rationally determined to be ultimate (in other words, "the best.") (If you found the ultimate frame of reference, how would you know? If the ultimacy of a frame of reference is to be determined rationally, it must be determined in relation to *some frame of reference.*)

4. **Stop seeking the ultimate spiritual practice.** Recognize that no spiritual practice can be rationally determined to be ultimate. (If you found the ultimate spiritual practice, how would you know, given that there can be no ultimate frame of reference?)

5. **Stop seeking the ultimate experience.** Recognize no experience can be rationally determined to be ultimate. (If you were having the ultimate experience, how would you know, given that there can be no ultimate frame of reference?)

6. **Relax your understanding of reality.** You've recognized that your perception of reality is defined by your worldview (which is a frame of reference) and that no frame of reference is ultimate. This frees you to be more open to alternative ways of understanding reality—ways that may differ from what you've been used to. You can hold divergent frameworks in mind to gain multiple perspectives on your experience—giving you multiple possible interpretations of phenomena—without having to reduce these divergent frameworks into a single master (ultimate) framework. Consider what worldviews you're most familiar with. (For in-

stance: scientific materialism? New age metaphysics?) Concept-focused perception in terms of these frameworks is a habit, and old habits die hard. Recognize when you're limiting yourself to familiar ways of making sense of life and make a conscious effort to expand your horizons. (If you come from a scientific materialist background, as I do, you may find the books by Dean Radin and Stanislav Grof listed in the bibliography helpful for exposing yourself to alternative worldviews.)

LIFE WITH NO ULTIMATE FRAME OF REFERENCE

How do we live life and make choices without an ultimate frame of reference to guide us? If you think you can simply do away with *all* frames of reference, good luck! (I doubt this would be possible or beneficial.) Instead, I like the idea of using frames of reference that are *appropriate for a given situation*—without making any one of them *ultimate*. (You can tell when you're making a frame of reference ultimate when you feel compelled to reduce all other ways of understanding life to *your way.*)

It may be tempting to view levels 1 through 6 of insight as a series of increasingly beneficial modes of perception; however, I doubt that this is a helpful perspective. I believe different modes of perception are appropriate for different situations. Perhaps our intention in cultivating insight should be to increase our perceptual *flexibility* rather than to remain in the more advanced states of insight at all times.

If we let go of the idea that we can find the ultimate frame of reference and use it to guide our lives—that is, if we stop *identifying* with our frames of reference and start taking them as *objects of attention*—it soon becomes clear that reason alone is inadequate for guiding our lives. That's because reason requires a frame of reference within which to operate; with no ultimate frame of reference, we can't look to reason alone for guidance. In particular, without the illusion of an ultimate frame of reference, reason is no longer helpful for evaluating which frames of reference are most appropriate to use in making sense of any given situation; we clearly need something else. However, there's nothing about the no-reference level that informs us what that *something else* must be.

That being said, personally, I've found intuition to be extremely helpful as an essential complement to reason. (I use the term *intuition* to encompass all non-rational forms of knowing and decision-making.) Reason is precise but slow; intuition, on the other hand, can quickly integrate vast expanses of conscious and unconscious phenomena to create an overall *intuitive hit* (that is, an intuitive knowing). Intuition is our built-in analog computer.

Here's a brief summary of how I currently live my life and how intuition fits in. I view life as a balancing act. Periodically, I get an uneasy feeling that "something's off;" this is an indication of *imbalance*. When I sense imbalance, I mindfully expand my field of attention to include that feeling and all other relevant experiences; then I let reason and intuition do their thing. Eventually, the uneasy feeling dissipates, I usually learn something, and it becomes clear what to do next. I do it; this action is my attempt to address the imbalance. After I act, I eventually become aware of additional imbalances—and the cycle continues.

This way of life is like standing on one foot—I'm constantly in motion, life is never completely in balance, and my attempts to address imbalance sometimes create more problems. Nothing is certain and there are no guarantees.

SIGNS OF NO REFERENCE

What are the signs that you are starting to access a state of no reference? One sign is the dropping away of zeal, defensiveness, and sanctimoniousness in relation to your preferred frames of reference. Another sign is an increase in your humility in relation to the finality or completeness of your spiritual development. (Be suspicious of any sense of certainty that you've arrived at an endpoint of your spiritual development; unqualified certainty suggests embeddedness in a frame of reference.)

For me, the results of this level of insight practice have included deepening levels of equanimity, humility, and conceptual flexibility, and an increasingly strong sense of "Uh... maybe! I don't know!" about every possible conceptual understanding. In the no-reference level of insight, what do I know for sure? Nothing! Am I certain that what I'm doing is right and good? No! Does that mean I sit around idly all day? No—I still do plenty; I just try to recognize (and drop) any sense of righteousness about what I'm doing. Why do I do what I do? I can give justifications relative to my preferred frames of reference, but I have no *ultimate* justification. Ultimately, I just don't know. It's turtles, all the way down.

Is my mind a pure, blank slate? No—I still think a lot, and I use frames of reference all the time; I'm just more *conscious* of them now. In fact, playing with frameworks is one of my favorite pastimes! Case in point: writing part 3 of this book—in doing so, my intention is to construct a frame of reference that efficiently creates an experience that I'm calling *insight*.

I'm also attempting to construct frames of reference that create experiences of vitality and mindfulness. Does that contradict what I'm teaching about this level of insight? No—this level of insight involves *disembedding* ourselves from all frames of reference, not *discarding* all frames of reference. Insight is distinct from nihilism and hedonism; these are frames of reference, like any other (and they aren't ones that appeal to me much). I still have opinions about what's good and bad; I just try to recognize them as *opinions based on my preferred frames of reference*. Would it be good if you adopted my preferred frames of reference? Relative to those frameworks: maybe. But ultimately: I don't know!

Is insight itself a good thing? Will it make you a better person and make the world a better place? Any definitive answer to these questions must depend on some frame of reference; without an ultimate frame of reference, there's no ultimate answer. My advice to you: only start cultivating this level of insight if you're willing to let go of your certainty about *everything* you currently understand to be true.

IN OTHER FRAMEWORKS

The no-reference level of insight seems related to the *Heart Sutra* in Mahayana Buddhism and developmental psychologist Robert Kegan's concept of the *self-transforming mind* as described in his book *Immunity to Change*.

The concepts of *intuition* and *balance* seem related to the concept of *Tao* in Taoism.

INSIGHT AS FREEDOM

Let's face it—for most of us, cultivating insight requires a lot of work. If you want to *experience* the presence level and beyond (as opposed to just understanding them conceptually), you'll need to cultivate an intermediate level of concentration first. If you have other issues that make cultivating concentration more challenging —for instance, low vitality, a stressful life, or mental health issues— you may need to take steps to address these issues, as well. All in all, it's possible that your journey of cultivating insight could be a long one requiring a significant amount of energy and dedication. Not only that, but you will likely need to let go of some beliefs you hold dear, both about who you are and about the world you live in.

Is insight worth it? Only you can answer that question for yourself. For me, the answer is an unequivocal "yes!" If I could do it all over again, I would. (In fact, I do much of it over again in every good meditation session! Granted, the journey is much faster and easier now.) Together, mindfulness and insight are a powerful package and the life changes that are required for cultivating them are probably things you would want to do anyway to support your general health and well-being.

Insight frees us in a number of significant ways. It frees us from misconceptions about who we are, what we perceive, and our relationship to the world we live in; it frees us from fears of nonexistence; and it frees us from attachment to any particular way of making sense of life. Insight can free us from exploitation by others, as well; we're much harder to manipulate when we're no longer confined to any particular frame of reference. Free from the mistaken belief that reason alone was ever an adequate guide to living our lives, we can open ourselves to trans-rational ways of understanding and moving through life that are, in my experience, both more enjoyable and more effective. Once you get a taste of all these freedoms, there's no going back.

(Framing the quest for insight as a choice may be misleading. I believe it's possible that when we have reached a stage of development at which we are *ready* to cultivate insight, we are magnetically drawn *toward* the cultivation of insight—whether we like it or not! That certainly seemed to be the case for me.)

SUMMARY

The fifth level of insight unfolds as we try to examine the witness more closely. You can search your field of nonconceptual experience forever, and you will *never* find a nonconceptual experience of the witness. (We've defined the witness as an entity distinct from experience that does the experiencing. That means that no matter what nonconceptual experience we turn our attention to, we will always perceive that experience to be "not-witness;" it always seems that the witness must be something else.)

The witness—that which is aware—can't be found. But clearly, you're aware of your experiences. What's going on? Awareness and experience are two sides of the same coin; you can't have one without the other. The perceptual practice of this level of insight is to *let go* of the concept of the witness and recognize awareness as an integral aspect of *all* experience.

At this level, the absence of a witness lends a quality of *evenness* to experience and awareness (which is why I call this fifth level of insight the *evenness level).* Your awareness is present in all your experiences (as opposed to concentrated in a separate witness) and everywhere there is awareness, there is experience (your space of awareness is always completely filled with your experiences); experience and awareness always arise together.

We usually take it for granted that we're somewhere "in here," experiencing things "out there." Challenging this assumption through inquiry can be an effective way of cultivating the evenness level of insight; I call this practice *investigating your experience of self.*

In the sixth level of insight, we go a step further and let go of the distinction between awareness and experience—effectively doing away with the last vestige of a sense of awareness/self as something distinct from experience. (I call this the *experience-only level.)* In the state corresponding to this level, our experience of life is simply that of subjective experience arising, with no self to be found anywhere—not as the witness, nor as awareness.

A *frame of reference* (or *framework)* is a set of interrelated concepts that allows you to make sense of experience. In the seventh level of insight, which I call the *no-reference level,* we learn to recognize how frames of reference affect our perception and we realize that *no* frame of reference—not the frame of reference of the experience-only level, nor any other—can be rationally determined to be ultimate (that is, "the best").

You're *embedded* in a frame of reference when you experience your frame of reference as "the best" and alternative frames of reference as inferior or threatening. You can disembed yourself from frames of reference by understanding them, learning to recognize them, and becoming aware of how they affect your perception.

If we let go of the idea that we can find the ultimate frame of reference and use it to guide our lives—that is, if we stop *identifying with* our frames of reference and start taking them as *objects of attention*—it soon becomes clear that reason alone is inadequate for guiding our lives. That's because reason requires a frame of reference within which to operate; with no ultimate frame of reference, we can't look to reason alone for guidance. Personally, I've found intuition to be extremely helpful as a complement to reason. (I use the term *intuition* to encompass all non-rational forms of knowing and decision-making.) Intuition is our built-in analog computer.

Two signs that you're starting to access a state of no reference include the dropping away of zeal, defensiveness, and sanctimoniousness and an increase in your humility in relation to the finality or completeness of your spiritual development.

Insight frees us in many ways: it frees us from misconceptions about who we are, what we perceive, and our relationship to the world we live in; it frees us from fears of nonexistence; and it frees us from attachment to any particular way of making sense of life. Insight can free us from exploitation by others, as well. Free from the mistaken belief that reason alone was ever an adequate guide to living our lives, we can open ourselves to trans-rational ways of understanding and moving through life that are, in my experience, both more enjoyable and more effective.

EPILOGUE

I F YOU'VE CREATED a spiritual practice routine for yourself and started engaging in the mindfulness and insight practices I recommend in the previous chapters, then congratulations! You've embarked on a spiritual adventure that will likely be of great benefit to you and all other beings. This epilogue describes a few possible directions in which you might consider exploring as you continue your adventure.

This book can be viewed as a map of two facets of awakening: mindfulness and insight. After you become familiar with the territory described by this map—that is, after you've made some progress in cultivating mindfulness and insight—what might you do next? Here are some suggestions:

- **Keep practicing!** The process of awakening is never finished.
- **Connect with community.** If you haven't done so yet, connect with others who share your spiritual values and interests. This will accelerate your awakening and will give you an opportunity to contribute to the well-being of others, too. (You can connect with the Spiritual Awakening for Geeks community by visiting spiritualawakeningforgeeks.com.)
- **Explore mindfulness and insight further.** There's more to mindfulness and insight than what's described in this book— so, continue exploring *beyond* this book. See spiritualawakeningforgeeks.com for more resources for culti-

vating mindfulness and insight, and see the bibliography, which lists a number of additional resources that I've found helpful.

- **Explore additional aspects of awakening.** As I describe in the introduction, there's much more to awakening than cultivating mindfulness and insight. Personally, I've also found it helpful to cultivate emotional and social intelligence, vitality, and intuition. See spiritualawakeningforgeeks.com for resources for cultivating additional aspects of awakening.
- **Explore diverse maps of awakening.** Each map is a frame of reference. All frames of reference shine a light on some phenomena and cast a shadow on others. By familiarizing yourself with additional maps, you'll gradually get a more complete picture of the territory of awakening.
- **Go off-map.** If you explore beyond the edges of any map, you'll inevitably encounter new, unfamiliar phenomena. Explore this uncharted territory and make sense of it!
- **Create your own map.** These maps were not handed down by God; they were created by people like you and me, doing their spiritual practices and making sense of their experiences. Eventually, you may reach a point at which you're ready to reframe maps made by others or map previously uncharted territory—so, start creating *your own* maps! Then—if you're so inclined—share them with others, as I'm doing now.

For me, spiritual awakening has been (and continues to be) the ultimate adventure—and there's no end in sight.

Notes

Introduction

10 *philosopher Ken Wilber's Integral Theory:* Wilber, *Integral Spirituality,*
1-11.

10 *His work has also influenced my views on the evolution of consciousness:*
Ibid., chap. 2.

11 *Kenneth Folk has applied Ken Wilber's concept of quadrants to spiritual
awakening:* Folk, "Awakening Is Possible, But So What? A Pragmatic Approach to Intersubjective Awakening."

Part One: Prepare for the Journey

41 *As Buddhist teacher Ken McLeod has pointed out:* McLeod, *Wake Up To
Your Life,* 105-13.

Part Two: Cultivate Mindfulness

57 *B. Alan Wallace's work:* Wallace, *The Attention Revolution.*

88 *Ken Wilber has described meditation experiences like this as "being at the
movies:"* Wilber, *The Collected Works of Ken Wilber, Volume Four,*
357.

88 *Peter Levine's concept of pendulation:* Levine, *Healing Trauma,* 56-7.

90   *neuroscience researcher Willoughby Britton has cataloged:* Britton, "The Dark Side of Dharma;" and Britton, "The Dark Night Project."

98   *The expansiveness practices in this section have been informed by the published work of Buddhist teacher Ken McLeod:* for instance, McLeod, *Wake Up To Your Life,* 361-2.

PART THREE: CULTIVATE INSIGHT

107   *the published work of Buddhist teacher Ken McLeod:* McLeod, *Wake Up To Your Life,* chap. 9-10; McLeod, *Unfettered Mind: Pragmatic Buddhism.*

110   *Thanks to Ken Wilber for the transcend and include model:* Wilber, *Integral Spirituality,* 128.

126   *Ken Wilber's concept of flatland:* Wilber, *A Theory of Everything,* 86.

168   *Robert Kegan's concept of the self-transforming mind:* Kegan and Lahey, *Immunity to Change,* 53.

GLOSSARY

advanced concentration milestones. As you traverse the *advanced concentration milestones,* you learn to effortlessly maintain single-pointed attention. (See p. 94.) (Also see *concentration milestones* and *single-pointed attention.*) (The level of concentration corresponding to the advanced milestones seems related to the concept of *samadhi* in Buddhism.)

aspects of attention. Stability, clarity, expansiveness, and range; these determine the quality of your attention and thus your level of mindfulness. (See p. 56.) (Also see *stability, clarity, expansiveness, range, attention,* and *mindfulness.*)

attention. The mental faculty that supports selective awareness of your experiences. (See p. 56.) (Also see *field of experience.*)

awakening. (See *spiritual awakening.*)

awareness. Awareness can be considered an attribute of your relationship to an experience: your *awareness* of an experience is the degree to which you perceive it. (See p. 56.) At the witnessing and presence levels of insight, *awareness* can also be used as a synonym for the witness. At the evenness level of insight, *awareness* can also be used as a synonym for the luminosity of experience or the space in which experience arises. (Also see *field of experience, the witness, witnessing level, presence level, evenness level, luminosity of experience,* and *space of awareness.*)

beginning concentration milestones. As you traverse the *beginning concentration milestones* you are focused on building attentional stability;

you gradually address the problem of complete distraction. (See p. 64.) (Also see *concentration milestones, stability,* and *complete distraction.*)

chosen object of attention. Whatever you've been intending to pay attention to. (See p. 64.) (Also see *attention.*)

clarity. An aspect of attention. The *clarity of your attention* is your ability to bring vivid, continuous awareness to your experiences. (If attention were light, clarity would be the intensity and continuity of that light.) (See p. 57.) *Clarity of awareness* is what you get when you have clarity of attention. (See p. 57.) (Also see *attention, aspects of attention,* and *awareness.*)

complete distraction. In *complete distraction,* your attention gets completely drawn away from your chosen object of attention, and you completely forget about it for a while. (See p. 64.) (Also see *distraction, attention,* and *chosen object of attention.*)

complete dullness. In *complete dullness,* your awareness of your chosen object of attention periodically fades out completely. (See p. 70.) (Also see *dullness, awareness,* and *chosen object of attention.*)

concentration. A practice in which you intentionally direct and clarify your attention in order to cultivate attentional stability and clarity. Also, the spectrum of states of mind that result from this practice— states of mind characterized by increasingly stable, clear awareness. (See p. 59.) (Also see *stability, clarity, attention,* and *awareness.*) (The concept of *concentration* in this approach seems closely related to the Buddhist concepts of *samadhi* (concentration), *samatha* (calming the mind), *dhyana or jhana* (meditation), and *anapanasati* (mindfulness of breathing)).

concentration milestones. Four beginning milestones, three intermediate milestones, and two advanced milestones; these milestones guide you from complete distraction through beginning, intermediate, and advanced levels of concentration. (See p. 64.) (Also see *beginning concentration milestones, intermediate concentration milestones, advanced concentration milestones, complete distraction,* and *concentration.*)

concept-focused perception. Perception in which your attention is mainly on conceptual experiences, you may not be aware of your nonconceptual experiences, and you may not recognize your subjective experience *as* subjective experience. (See p. 120.) (Also see *conceptual experience* and *nonconceptual experience*.)

conceptual experience. An experience that involves concepts. For instance, when you see an elephant and the word *elephant* comes to mind, this is a conceptual experience (because it involves the concept *elephant*.) Likewise, when you hear the word *elephant* and an elephant comes to mind, this is also a conceptual experience. (See p. 47.) (Also see *experience* and *nonconceptual experience*.)

conceptual understanding. The process by which your subjective experience is transformed into conceptual knowledge via a frame of reference. (See p. 163.) (Also see *experience* and *frame of reference*.)

diagnosis. An approach to introspection in which you look for specific problems (such as distraction and dullness). (See p. 71.) (Also see *introspection, distraction,* and *dullness*.)

distraction. Occurs when your attention gets drawn away from your chosen object of attention. Distraction can be complete, partial, or subtle; these are on a continuum. (Also see *attention, chosen object of attention, complete distraction, partial distraction, subtle distraction,* and *dullness*.)

doing-nothing meditation. A type of formal meditation practice. Instructions: when you notice yourself trying to do *anything*—including trying to stop thinking—let go of the doing. (See p. 97.) (Also see *formal practice sessions*.)

dullness. Lack of vividness and fade-outs of awareness are due to *dullness* (lack of attentional clarity); when there's insufficient energy in your attention, your chosen object simply fades out of awareness. (The experience itself doesn't change; you just lose awareness of the experience.) If your attention were a beam of light, dullness would be a condition where the light source has insufficient power and periodically grows dimmer. (This is different from distraction, in which the beam shifts direction to illuminate something other than your chosen object.) Dullness can be complete, partial, or subtle; these are on a continuum. (See p. 70.) (Also see *fade-out, clarity, chosen object of attention, distraction, complete dullness, partial dullness,* and *subtle dullness.*)

edge level. The level of insight that's your current edge for growth. (See p. 130.) (Also see *levels of insight.*)

edge state. The state of mind corresponding to your edge level of insight. (See p. 130.) (Also see *edge level.*)

embedded. You're embedded in a frame of reference when you experience your frame of reference as "the best" and alternative frames of reference (with competing concepts) as inferior or threatening; this makes it difficult or impossible for you to use alternative frames of reference to make sense of your experience. (See p. 162.) (Also see *frame of reference.*)

energetic aspect of breathing. In physics, *energy* refers to the ability of a system to perform work. Around the third and fourth concentration milestones, I often start noticing the sensations of a phenomenon that seems to be driving the work of breathing; I call this phenomenon the *energetic aspect of breathing.* These energetic sensations are distinct from the tactile sensations of breathing; the tactile sensations include the feeling of your muscles moving and the feeling of air moving against your skin, while the energetic sensations include more diffuse, wave-like sensations related to the urge (or impulse) to breathe in and out. (See p. 75.)

evenness. The state of mind corresponding to the evenness level of insight. At the evenness level of insight, the absence of a witness lends a quality of *evenness* to experience and awareness: your awareness is present in *all* your experiences (as opposed to concentrated in a separate witness) and everywhere there is awareness, there is experience (your space of awareness is always completely filled with your experiences); experience and awareness always arise together. (See p. 118.) (Also see *experience, awareness, the witness,* and *evenness level.*)

evenness level. The fifth level of insight, at which you recognize the unity of awareness and experience. Evenness of awareness and experience, the luminosity of experience, and the space of awareness become apparent at this level. (See p. 151.) (Also see *levels of insight, evenness, luminosity of experience,* and *space of awareness.*)

expansiveness. An aspect of attention. The *expansiveness of your attention* is your ability to expand your attentional "field of view" to attend to many experiences simultaneously. (If attention were a beam of light, expansiveness would be your ability to widen that beam.) (See p. 57.) *Expansiveness of awareness* is what you get when you have expansiveness of attention. (See p. 57.) (Also see *attention, aspects of attention,* and *awareness.*)

expansiveness practices. Practices for cultivating attentional expansiveness. (See p. 98.) (Also see *expansiveness, spiritual practice.*)

experience. (Also *subjective experience.*) What happens when you're aware of anything. For instance, when I look out my window, I have an experience of a tree; when I attend to my feeling state, I have an experience of tiredness. (See p. 47.) (Also see *field of experience.*)

experience-focused perception. Perception in which your attention encompasses both your nonconceptual and conceptual experiences and you recognize your subjective experience *as* subjective experience. (See p. 120.) (Also see *conceptual experience* and *nonconceptual experience.*)

experience-only level. The sixth level of insight, at which we let go of the distinction between awareness and experience. (See p. 159.) (Also see *levels of insight, awareness,* and *experience.*)

facets of awakening. Measures of awakening, faculties that result from awakening, and catalysts for further awakening. For instance, vitality, mindfulness, and insight. In my model of awakening, facets of awakening are the top-level categories that I use to conceptualize awakening and to organize spiritual practices. (See p. 11.) (Also see *spiritual awakening, mindfulness, insight,* and *vitality.*)

fade-out. When you're attending to your chosen object, if you look closely, you'll notice that your experience of it fades in and out—occasionally fading out completely. (The experience itself doesn't change; you just lose awareness of the experience.) The *fade-out* may last anywhere from a fraction of a second to several seconds or more. (See p. 70.) (Also see *chosen object of attention and dullness.*)

field of experience. Your *field of experience* is the set of all your current subjective experiences. (This is actually more like a field or a space than
a set, since experiences aren't distinct units with clear boundaries.)
Think of your field of experience as a vast landscape of experiences,
and your attention as light shining on that landscape. At any given
time, depending on what the light is doing, some parts of that landscape will be well lit, others will be dimly lit, and others will be in
shadows. Likewise, at any given time, depending on what your attention is doing, you'll have a clear awareness of some of your experiences, you'll have less awareness of others, and you'll hardly be
aware of other experiences at all. (See p. 55.) (Also see *experience, attention, awareness,* and *space of awareness.*)

field of view. Your attentional *field of view* is the portion of your field of
experience that you currently have a clear awareness of. (See p. 56.)
(Also see *field of experience.*)

formal practice sessions. Times set aside specifically for meditation or
other forms of spiritual practice. (See p. 34.) (Also see *meditation,
spiritual practice,* and *informal practice.*)

frame of reference (or **framework**). A set of interrelated concepts that allows you to make sense of experience. Belief systems, conceptual
models, and worldviews are all examples of frames of reference. (See
p. 160.) (Also see *experience* and *worldview.*)

framework. (See *frame of reference.*)

informal practice. Spiritual practices interspersed in daily life; for instance,
a mindfulness practice such as noticing the sound of the rain on the
roof as you cook dinner. (See p. 34.) (Also see *spiritual practice* and
formal practice sessions.)

insight. The result of insight practice; an understanding of the relationships between self, reality, awareness, and subjective experience—
and an ability to access modes of perception in which those relationships are evident. (See p. 107.) (Also see *insight practice, awareness*
and *experience.*) (The concept of *insight,* as I've defined it, seems
closely related to the concept of *vipassana* or *vipasyana*—often translated as *insight*—in Buddhism.)

insight practice. The experiential exploration of the relationships between self, reality, awareness, and subjective experience. (See p. 107.) (Also see *awareness, experience,* and *insight.*)

interdependence level. The second level of insight, at which you perceive yourself *as* reality—*all of* reality. (See p. 117.) (Also see *levels of insight* and *reality.*)

interdependent self. The self you perceive at the interdependence level of insight. (See p. 118.) (Also see *interdependence level.*)

intermediate concentration milestones. As you traverse the *intermediate concentration milestones,* you learn how to overcome partial distraction and partial dullness. (See p. 82.) (Also see *concentration milestones, partial distraction,* and *partial dullness.*) (The level of concentration corresponding to the intermediate milestones seems related to the concept of *access concentration* in Theravada Buddhism.)

introspection. When you notice that you've been lost in thought, you've exercised a capacity called *introspection* which allows you to examine or scrutinize what's going on in your mind. Introspection is how you make unconscious mental processes conscious; it increases your level of mindfulness by expanding the range of your attention and awareness to include these mental processes. (See p. 70.) (Also see *mindfulness* and *range.)* (Using introspection to scrutinize the act of thinking seems related to the concept of *metacognition* in psychology.)

intuition. I use this term to encompass all non-rational forms of knowing and decision-making. (See p. 166.)

levels of insight. A series of seven levels over which understanding and perception become successively more refined. Each level has a corresponding conceptual framework (or *view*) as well as a corresponding perceptual state (that can be entered by using the associated view to guide your perception). (See p. 111.) (Also see *insight, view, reality level, interdependence level, witnessing level, presence level, evenness level, experience-only level,* and *no-reference level.*)

luminosity of experience. The "glow" of awareness that becomes apparent as an inseparable aspect of all experiences at the evenness level of insight. (See p. 154.) (Also see *awareness, experience,* and *evenness level.*)

meditation. Any practice that involves directing your attention toward your current subjective experiences. (See p. 23.) (Also see *attention* and *experience.*)

milestone. (See *concentration milestones.*)

mindfulness. Awareness of your field of experience; equivalently, awareness of your current experiences. (See p. 56.) Or, more precisely, a stable, clear, expansive awareness of a wide range of your current experiences. (See p. 57.) A facet of awakening. (Also see *field of experience, experience, stability, clarity, expansiveness, range,* and *facets of awakening.*) (In other frameworks, I've seen the term *mindfulness* used in a variety of ways; this can be confusing, so when in doubt, ask for a definition. The concept of *mindfulness* in this framework seems related to the concept of *mindfulness* in psychology. The concept of *sati* in Buddhism—often translated as *mindfulness* or *awareness*—might be described as *mindfulness with moral discernment* in the lexicon of this framework.)

mindfulness chaining. An informal mindfulness practice in which you ask yourself what you need to do next, choose a small task that will take a minute or less to complete, and set an intention to stay mindful (that is, to maintain a stable, clear, expansive awareness of a wide range of your current experiences) *as* you do that task. As soon as that task is complete, you immediately repeat this process. (See p. 101.) (Also see *mindfulness* and *informal practice.*)

nonconceptual experience. An experience that doesn't involve concepts. For instance, when you look at (or imagine) an elephant and simply notice its visual appearance—without putting words to that appearance—this is a nonconceptual experience. (See p. 47.) (Also see *experience* and *conceptual experience.*)

no-reference level. The seventh level of insight, at which we learn to recognize how frames of reference affect our perception and we realize that no frame of reference can be rationally determined to be ultimate. (See p. 161.) (Also see *levels of insight* and *frame of reference.*)

noting. A technique in which you name what you're trying to notice as soon as you notice it. This simple act of naming helps bring that phenomenon more solidly into consciousness and helps you recognize that phenomenon more easily the next time it shows up. Noting increases your level of mindfulness by expanding the range of your attention and awareness. (See p. 71.) (Also see *mindfulness* and *range.*)

partial distraction. Occurs when something distracts you from your chosen object and most of your attention shifts to what's distracting you —but your attention never *completely* leaves your chosen object. (So you end up with *most* of your attention on what's distracting you and *some* of your attention on your chosen object.) (See p. 69.) (Also see *distraction, attention,* and *chosen object of attention.*)

partial dullness. In *partial dullness,* your awareness of your chosen object periodically fades out partially, but not completely. (See p. 81.) (Also see *dullness, awareness,* and *chosen object of attention.*)

pointing out. In insight practice, an important function of a spiritual mentor or teacher is *pointing out* states of insight; this involves creating the conditions for states of insight to arise and helping you recognize them when they do. (See p. 132.) (Also see *insight.*)

presence level. The fourth level of insight, in which our relationship to reality shifts and present-moment subjective experience assumes a much more prominent role. (See p. 120.) (Also see *levels of insight, reality,* and *experience.*)

presence. The state of mind corresponding to the presence level of insight. (Also see *presence level.*)

range. An aspect of attention; the *range of your attention* is your ability to attend to a diversity of experiences. For instance, if you find thinking easy but identifying feelings difficult, your attentional range would be weighted toward thoughts and away from feelings. (If attention were light and your experiences were spread across a landscape, your attentional range would correspond to the portion of the landscape that you're able to light up.) (See p. 57.) *Range of awareness* is what you get when you have range of attention. (See p. 57.) (Also see *attention, aspects of attention,* and *awareness.*)

range practices. Practices for cultivating attentional range. (See p. 98.) (Also see *range, spiritual practice*.)

reality. The set of phenomena perceived both by you and by others who share your worldview. (See p. 115.) (Also see *worldview*.)

reality level. The first level of insight, at which you perceive yourself to be a part of reality. (See p. 116.) (Also see *levels of insight* and *reality*.)

real self. The self you perceive at the reality level of insight. (The *real* in *real self* means "associated with reality"—not "genuine.") (See p. 118.) (Also see *reality level*.)

remembering the goal. An approach to introspection in which you remember or imagine the state of mind you want to be in and notice differences between your current state of mind and this goal state. (See p. 71.) (Also see *introspection*.)

retreat. An extended period of time reserved for spiritual practice—*extended* meaning longer than what's usual for you in your daily practice routine. (See p. 35.) (Also see *spiritual practice* and *spiritual practice routine*.)

sign. Around the fourth concentration milestone, many people (but not all) start noticing an unusual visual phenomenon that starts showing up in the visual field during meditation. It can appear whether your eyes are open or closed. I call this phenomenon the *sign*. (See p. 76.) (Also see *concentration milestones*.) (This phenomenon seems related to the concept of the *counterpart sign* or the *nimitta* in Buddhism.)

single-pointed attention. Attention that's completely stable and clear. (See p. 93.) (Also see *attention, stability*, and *clarity*.)

space of awareness. When you conceive of experience as an inseparable aspect of awareness (at the evenness level of insight), your awareness seems like a space filled with your experiences—the *space of awareness*. (Equivalent to your *field of experience*.) (See p. 154.) (Also see *awareness, evenness level*, and *field of experience*.)

spiritual awakening. The evolution of consciousness toward greater wisdom and compassion. As we awaken, we grow both more empowered and more likely to use our power for good. We grow both more able and more willing to serve the well-being of all. (See p. 8.) If spiritual awakening is a process of evolution, then we can define *a spiritual awakening* as a *step* in that process. A spiritual awakening is a qualitative (rather than a quantitative) shift in consciousness—usually, a shift that's experienced for the first time. (See p. 10.)

Spiritual Awakening for Geeks. A project that includes an approach to awakening (that's intended to be clear, coherent, and practical, and that's not associated with any particular religion or spiritual tradition) and a community (that's organized around this approach). (See p. 2.) (Also see *spiritual awakening*.)

spiritual practice. An activity that you engage in to help you awaken. (See p. 19.) (Also see *spiritual awakening*.)

spiritual practice routine. A set of spiritual practices that you make a habit of doing regularly. (See p. 19.) (Also see *spiritual practice*.)

stability. An aspect of attention. The *stability of your attention* is your capacity to pay attention to what you choose to, without getting distracted. (If attention were light, stability would be your ability to direct that light.) Without stability, your attention is easily diverted into involuntary thinking. (See p. 57.) *Stability of awareness* is what you get when you have stability of attention. (See p. 57.) (Also see *attention, aspects of attention,* and *awareness*.)

subjective experience. (See *experience*.)

subtle distraction. Distraction in which *most* of your attention is on your chosen object and *some* of your attention is on what's distracting you. (See p. 85.) (Also see *distraction, attention,* and *chosen object of attention*.)

subtle dullness. Occasional, barely perceptible fade-outs of your awareness of your chosen object. (See p. 86.) (Also see *dullness, awareness,* and *chosen object of attention*.)

view. Each level of insight has a corresponding conceptual framework (or *view*). (See p. 111.) (Also see *levels of insight* and *frame of reference*.)

vitality. Well-being, experienced as a sense of relaxed, energized openness. (See p. 17.) A facet of awakening. (Also see *facets of awakening*.) (The concept of *vitality* in Spiritual Awakening for Geeks seems related to the concept of *virya or viriya*—often translated as energy, diligence, enthusiasm, or effort—in Buddhism.)

the witness. In the witnessing level of insight: that which is aware. (See p. 119.) (Also see *awareness* and *witnessing level.*)

witnessing level. The third level of insight, at which you perceive yourself as the witness of phenomena. (See p. 119.) (Also see *levels of insight* and *the witness.*)

worldview. A set of interrelated concepts (a frame of reference) that supports your perception of reality. (See p. 115.) (Also see *frame of reference* and *reality.*)

Bibliography

Adyashanti. *The End of Your World: Uncensored Straight Talk on the Nature of Enlightenment*. Boulder, Colo.; Enfield: Sounds True, 2010.

Brasington, Leigh. "Instructions for Entering Jhana." *Insight Journal*, Fall 2002. https://www.bcbsdharma.org/article/instructions-for-entering-jhana/.

Britton, Willoughby. "The Dark Night Project." Interview by Vincent Horn. *Buddhist Geeks*, audio recording, n.d. https://soundcloud.com/buddhistgeeks/the-dark-night-project.

———. "The Dark Side of Dharma." Interview by Vincent Horn. *Buddhist Geeks*, audio recording, n.d. https://soundcloud.com/buddhistgeeks/the-dark-side-of-dharma.

Catherine, Shaila. "Establishing Concentration through Mindfulness with Breathing." Sec. 1 in *Wisdom Wide and Deep: A Practical Handbook for Mastering Jhana and Vipassana*. Boston: Wisdom Publications, 2011.

Folk, Kenneth. "Awakening Is Possible, But So What? A Pragmatic Approach to Intersubjective Awakening." Interview by Terry Patten. *Beyond Awakening*, audio recording, September 8, 2013. http://www.beyondawakeningseries.com/archive/.

Gotwals, Jacob. *Tricksters in the Desert: My Spiritual Journey from Skeptic to Buddhist and Beyond*. Albuquerque: Skyway Press, 2013.

Grof, Stanislav, and Hal Zina Bennett. *The Holotropic Mind: The Three Levels of Human Consciousness and How They Shape Our Lives*. Reprint edition. San Francisco, Calif: HarperOne, 1993. See esp. part 3, "The Transpersonal Paradigm."

Gyamtso, Khenpo Tsultrim. *Progressive Stages of Meditation on Emptiness.* New edition. Auckland, N.Z.: Zhyisil Chokyi Publications, 2001.

Ingram, Daniel M. "The Concentration States (Samatha Jhanas)." Chap. 21 in *Mastering the Core Teachings of the Buddha: An Unusually Hardcore Dharma Book.* London: Aeon Books, 2008.

Keeney, Bradford. *Shaking Medicine: The Healing Power of Ecstatic Movement.* Rochester, VT: Destiny Books, 2007.

———. *The Bushman Way of Tracking God: The Original Spirituality of the Kalahari People.* New York / Hillsboro, OR: Atria Books/Beyond Words, 2010.

Kegan, Robert, and Lisa Laskow Lahey. Chap. 1-2 in *Immunity to Change: How to Overcome It and Unlock the Potential in Yourself and Your Organization.* Boston, Mass: Harvard Business Review Press, 2009. See esp. figures 1-7 and 2-6.

Kornfield, Jack. *A Path with Heart: A Guide Through the Perils and Promises of Spiritual Life.* New York, NY: Bantam, 1993.

Levine, Peter A. *Healing Trauma: A Pioneering Program for Restoring the Wisdom of Your Body.* Boulder (Colorado): Sounds True, 2008.

Maharshi, Sri Ramana. *Be as You Are: The Teachings of Sri Ramana Maharshi.* Edited by David Godman. Reissue edition. London: Penguin Books, 1989.

McLeod, Ken. "Dismantling Attachment to Conventional Success," "Insight and Dismantling Illusion," and "No Separation." Chap. 4, 9, and 10 in *Wake Up To Your Life: Discovering the Buddhist Path of Attention.* San Francisco: HarperOne, 2002.

———. *Unfettered Mind: Pragmatic Buddhism.* Audio recordings of Ken McLeod's retreat and workshop talks at http://unfetteredmind.org/.

Namgyal, Dakpo Tashi. *Clarifying the Natural State: A Principal Guidance Manual for Mahamudra.* Translated by Erik Pema Kunsang. Hong Kong: Rangjung Yeshe Publications, 2004.

Rabjam, Longchen. *The Precious Treasury of The Basic Space of Phenomena.* Translated by Richard Barron. Junction City, Calif: Padma Pub, 2001.

Radin, Dean. *The Conscious Universe: The Scientific Truth of Psychic Phenomena*. Reprint edition. New York: HarperOne, 2009.

Thrangu Rinpoche, Khenchen. *Crystal Clear: Practical Advice for Mahamudra Meditators*. Translated by Erik Pema Kunsang. Hong Kong: Rangjung Yeshe Publications, 2004.

————. *Pointing Out the Dharmakaya: Teachings on the Ninth Karmapa's Text*. 2nd edition. Ithaca: Snow Lion, 2012.

Urgyen Rinpoche, Tulku. *As It Is, Vol. 2*. Translated by Erik Pema Kunsang. Hong Kong: Rangjung Yeshe Publications, 2000.

Wallace, B. Alan. *The Attention Revolution: Unlocking the Power of the Focused Mind*. Boston: Wisdom Publications, 2006.

Wilber, Ken. *Integral Spirituality: A Startling New Role for Religion in the Modern and Postmodern World*. Boston: Shambhala, 2006.

————. "Stages of Meditation: An Interview with Ken Wilber." In *The Collected Works of Ken Wilber, Volume Four*, 356-62. Boston: Shambhala, 1999.

————. *A Theory of Everything: An Integral Vision for Business, Politics, Science and Spirituality*. Boston, Massachussets: Shambhala, 2001.

ABOUT THE AUTHOR

I LOVE TO LEARN how things work and create, design, and build systems; I've been doing that all my life, and I doubt I'll ever stop. I'm also fascinated by psychology, consciousness, personal growth and healing, and spiritual awakening.

GEEK

As a child, I loved video games, science fiction, and weather. In high school, when home computers came out in the 1980s, I was magnetically attracted to them. I wrote video games in BASIC and assembly language for friends and classmates. Later, I studied computer science—first at Swarthmore, then at Indiana University, where I got a PhD.

Determined to land a job in the high-tech mecca of Silicon Valley, I eventually ended up in the semiconductor industry developing software performance tools. After six years learning the ins and outs of corporate life, I moved to Albuquerque in search of a slower pace of life, better dating, and bigger thunderstorms. A few years later, I left the semiconductor industry seeking more time for spiritual practice.

Spiritual Explorer

In my early 30s, I discovered philosopher Ken Wilber. His work helped me break out of my scientific materialist shell, and his Integral framework was a helpful guide as I started exploring meditation and mystical spirituality.

Determined to access spiritual insight, I explored many spiritual traditions and communities looking for a good place to "go deep". Eventually, I settled into a local Tibetan Buddhist center (Albuquerque Karma Thegsum Choling, an affiliate center of Karma Triyana Dharmachakra). With a lot of study, practice, and guidance, I started to awaken to new ways of experiencing life. This awakening deepened as I shifted my attention to the Buddhist teachings of Ken McLeod and (later) Kenneth Folk.

Eventually, having found the insight I'd been looking for, I let go of my focus on Buddhism. As of this writing, I'm not affiliated with any particular religion or spiritual approach; my spiritual life is guided by an inner knowing and informed by a wide range approaches. I continue to seek deeper levels of awakening and ways to integrate awakening more deeply into my life. I describe my journey of awakening—and some lessons learned along the way—in my short book *Tricksters in the Desert*.

Psychotherapist

I enjoyed psychology courses as an undergraduate and considered pursuing a career in psychotherapy at that time; however, I ended up choosing to pursue my passion for technology, instead. Years later, after my high-tech career had wound down and my hunger for spiritual insight had been satisfied, I found my interests and career life circling back to psychotherapy and I completed a master's degree in counseling at Southwestern College in Santa Fe.

I'm living proof that spiritual insight does not automatically perfect the personality. The good news is that mindfulness and insight are great complements to other types of inner work (like building self-awareness, building social and emotional intelligence, and healing emotional wounds). I enjoy facilitating this type of inner work with others as a psychotherapist.

As of this writing, I live in Santa Fe, New Mexico with my wife Emilah DeToro and our furry "kids" Dora, Maisy, and Manu. To learn about my latest projects, visit jacobgotwals.com.

www.ingramcontent.com/pod-product-compliance
Lightning Source LLC
Chambersburg PA
CBHW030927090426
42737CB00007B/350